SONS OF GOD

A Study on the Biblical Narrative of the Sons of God

C. ORVILLE MCLEISH

Published by:

ISBN: 978-1-958404-73-7 (paperback)

FOREWORD

"Sons of God: A Study on the Biblical Narrative of the Sons of God" is a refreshing perspective on the nature of our existence and our relationship with the divine.

The book serves as a guide, offering insights and wisdom to those who seek a deeper connection with their spiritual selves. It delves into the concept of being children of God, highlighting the notion that we are not separate from the divine but rather an intrinsic part of its existence.

From a mystic perspective, the book helps readers understand their rightful place in Christ and invites them to tap into their innate divinity and align their thoughts, intentions, and actions with the Father.

Sons of God is not just a theoretical exploration of our divine nature but a practical manual for spiritual growth and awakening. It invites readers to experience a direct connection with the divine and to transcend the limitations of ordinary existence. It is a testament to the transformative power of embracing our inner divinity and living our lives in alignment with the greater truths of what the Bible says about us.

Embrace the teachings within these pages with an open heart and a willingness to embark on a journey of identity and spiritual awakening.

May this book serve as a guiding light, illuminating your path and revealing the boundless depths of your own divinity.

Pastor Robert Smith &
Minister Nickeisha Smith

ABOUT THE AUTHOR

C. Orville McLeish is an entrepreneur and devoted scholar of Scripture and mystical theology. He has transcended the ordinary to discover extraordinary dimensions of faith and identity. Prior to encountering Jesus Christ, he lived in relative anonymity, but the transformative encounter with his true identity as a redeemed human being, a cherished son of the Most High God, propelled him into a remarkable journey.

The revelation of his identity in Christ became the catalyst for profound change, shaping his life, ministry, and business in ways he could never have anticipated. His initiation into a supernatural reality was just the beginning. As he delved deeper into the mysteries of faith, God opened the portals of knowledge to him, unveiling the profound concept of oneness and union with the divine.

Today, he is much more than an entrepreneur; he is a chronicler of his extraordinary faith journey. In the pages of his writings, he shares a mere glimpse of the vast knowledge he has acquired. His life embodies the profound love of God that echoes through the annals of history, offering hope and resilience in every challenge he faces.

C. Orville McLeish invites readers to join him on a transformative exploration of faith, identity, and the mystical union with God. His words resonate with the power of personal experience and years of study and accumulated knowledge, offering a compelling narrative that extends an open invitation to all who seek deeper understanding. As an entrepreneur, scholar, and faithful witness, he exemplifies the enduring spirit encapsulated in the phrase that has guided his own journey: *"Never give up; You are born to win."*

ENDORSEMENTS

"

In "Sons of God," C. Orville McLeish embarks on an extraordinary exploration of divine kinship, inviting us into a profound understanding of what it means to be called children of the Most High. Anchored by the illuminating passage of First John 3:2, McLeish unravels the Biblical narrative with the precision of a theologian and the insight of a true scholar.

This book is an invitation to experience the likeness of our Creator and to function with divine purpose within the earth realm. McLeish's writing is empowered by a palpable recognition of our divine heritage and a lucid explanation of our earthly mission. His statement, *"Christianity was meant to be rooted in the reality of the incarnation: God becoming man; God becoming you,"* captures the essence of our faith with an eloquent simplicity that is both profound and accessible.

"Sons of God" is not merely informative; it is transformative. It challenges the reader to embrace the paradox of our existence: that while we are not God, God is integrally a part of us, as a painter is present in every stroke of the brush. This work is a clarion call to all believers to rise to the fullness of their identity as children of God.

As a fellow servant in ministry and a passionate advocate for deepening our understanding of the Scriptures, I wholeheartedly endorse this transformative work. "Sons of God" is a beacon of light, revealing our place in the divine tapestry with clarity and promise.

Kenneth D. Davis
Pastor
Empowered Outreach Church
Denton, Texas

"

I believe this is Minister Cleve's best work yet. Filled with hard-hitting, thought-provoking truth that will drive you into God's presence. Understanding who we are in this post-modern time is critical for the life and continual victory of every believer.

I have read it and will read it again; you won't be able to put it down.

Apostle Dino B. Nicholas
Founder, Harvest Manna Ministries
Senior Pastor

Beloved, we are [even here and] now God's children; it is not yet disclosed (made clear) what we shall be [hereafter], but we know that when He comes and is manifested, we shall [as God's children] resemble and be like Him, for we shall see Him just as He [really] is. (I John 3:2 - AMPC).

Jesus answered, is it not written in your Law, I said, You are gods? So men are called gods [by the Law], men to whom God's message came—and the Scripture cannot be set aside or cancelled or broken or annulled—[If that is true] do you say of the One Whom the Father consecrated and dedicated and set apart for Himself and sent into the world, You are blaspheming, because I said, I am the Son of God? (John 10:34-36 - AMPC).

TABLE OF CONTENTS

Foreword.. v

About the Author.. vii

Endorsements ix

Introduction 19

Revealing the Sons of God................................... 23

Preface 25

Chapter 1: Love Beyond..................................... 33

Chapter 2: Original Intent................................... 47

Chapter 3: The Garden of Eden........................... 61

Chapter 4: The Power of One............................... 77

Chapter 5: Perception Versus Reality.................... 87

Chapter 6: Build Me A House 103

Chapter 7: Manifesting God 109

Chapter 8: What is Man?.................................... 117

Chapter 9: The Sin Remover 133

Chapter 10: The Transmutational Power of the Believer.............. 139

Chapter 11: Thieves, Killers, Accusers, Liars, and Destroyers Seeking Refuge... 147

Chapter 12: Living the Ascended Life 157

Chapter 13: As He Is 171

Chapter 14: Key to Immortality 181

Conclusion.. 189

Fear is the belief that I have no power.

—-Anonymous

INTRODUCTION

I have been on a journey to untether from religion and unbelief to embrace a more authentic and organic relationship with the divine, and I have been exposed to high levels of spiritual knowledge via my mentor, etc., but this book stretched me a little bit because I am still somewhat entrenched in a predominantly religious culture, in a very religious nation. When I was instructed to write, I so wanted to escape this that I pulled up a few projects I had put on the back burner and tried working on them, but nothing was flowing, and I had no peace.

To be safe and balanced, I am careful to clarify a few things before I even begin this discourse so no one who reads this book can misquote or misjudge me on certain matters, even though that may still be the case.

I do not believe we are God. There is just one true living God, and that is YHVH (Yahweh). I call Him *Abba, Father.* There is none above or equal to Him, none that can dethrone Him, and none that can take His place. He is unshakable, immovable, self-existing, and will forever be the one, true living God.

I believe in Jesus Christ as the Son of God, the Word that existed in the beginning, the Word that became flesh and dwelt among us. I believe He came to earth, suffered, died, was resurrected, and ascended to the right hand of the Father. I believe He was given a name above all other names, and at His name, every knee will bow, and every tongue confess that He is Lord. Those who believe in Jesus are merged into Him as one entity, thereby becoming a son of God with a seemingly separate consciousness.

God only made one Adam and one woman, with the capacity to multiply themselves across the created world. We call it reproduction. If this is the case with the first Adam, it means the second Adam must also have the capacity to reproduce Himself across the created world.

And so it is written, "The first man Adam became a living being." The last Adam became a life-giving spirit. (1 Corinthians 15:45 - NKJV).

There is a certain interconnectedness with humanity and God that I think we miss, but we will talk about that in another book. There is already a lot to discuss and a lot to consider as we delve into this topic.

I believe in the Holy Spirit who was sent after Jesus ascended on the day of Pentecost. He is our Helper, Comforter, Master Teacher, and Guide. We are nothing without Him, and in Him, we are given access to the most potent power in all existence. He also opens up the realms of infinite knowledge, most of which humanity is still unable to bear, so much remains still a mystery.

I believe the Bible is the inspired written Word of God. The only difference is, when it speaks about "all scripture" in Timothy, I also believe this includes books that were not canonized, for example, the book of Enoch. I believe God will hide certain things until it is the right time for them to be revealed, and we must be open to that. It was God who said, **"I am doing a new thing." (see Isaiah 43:19).** There is no guarantee that God will do the same thing, the same way every time. That is a human thing. God is infinite and without limits.

I believe Jesus Christ is the living Word of God. He is alive. He speaks, listens, acts, visits, and engages with us. It is good to read the inspired Word, but we must also engage with the living Word. You cannot have a relationship with a book, but you can have one with the person of Jesus Christ.

I believe that only through the blood and body of Jesus, through redemption and salvation, can we access who we were meant to be from the very beginning. There is no other way. Every other way leads to a minuscule version of what is, but Jesus is the only Way, Truth and Life and all that God meant for the human being when He said, **"Let us make man…" (see Genesis 1:26).**

So now that I have laid that foundation, let us have a real conversation. Think not for one minute that I have all the answers you may be seeking. I do not. I have more questions than answers, but I do know a little bit because I subjected myself to be taught about things I knew nothing about. Religion can make you think you know everything, when in reality, you know nothing.

I do ask that you keep an open mind as you progress through this book, especially those who are still entrenched in religion who have the courage to take this book up and try to read it. I understand your struggles. I have been there. You are powerful, and you are brave to hold this book in your hand. There are those who won't, but I am consoled by the fact that this book was not meant for them.

REVEALING THE SONS OF GOD

For all who are led by the Spirit of God are sons of God. (Romans 8:14 - AMPC).

For [even the whole] creation (all nature) waits expectantly and longs earnestly for God's sons to be made known [waits for the revealing, the disclosing of their sonship]. (Romans 8:19 - AMPC).

And not only the creation, but we ourselves too, who have and enjoy the firstfruits of the [Holy] Spirit [a foretaste of the blissful things to come] groan inwardly as we wait for the redemption of our bodies [from sensuality and the grave, which will reveal] our adoption (our manifestation as God's sons). (Romans 8:23 - AMPC).

For in Christ Jesus you are all sons of God through faith. (Galatians 3:26 - AMPC).

And because you [really] are [His] sons, God has sent the [Holy] Spirit of His Son into our hearts, crying, Abba (Father)! Father! (Galatians 4:6 - AMPC).

Beloved, we are [even here and] now God's children; it is not yet disclosed (made clear) what we shall be [hereafter], but we know that when He comes and is manifested, we shall [as God's children] resemble and be like Him, for we shall see Him just as He [really] is. (1 John 3:2 - AMPC).

PREFACE

The revealing of humanity is the revealing of the One who created humanity because man was made in the image and likeness of God. The Bible is a revelation of the man-God, of God as Spirit becoming God in the flesh.

It means the revelation of Jesus is the revealing of our original estate, which is why He becomes the Way, Truth and Life, and there is no other way. We look at Jesus to see what the man in God is becoming; we look at Jesus to see what the man in God can do. Yes, we can look at the prophets and all those who moved in the Spirit, but they were all doing what Jesus did or would do.

So here we get an understanding of this verse:

Most assuredly, I say to you, he who believes in Me, the works that I do he will do also; and greater works than these he will do, because I go to My Father. (John 14:12 - NKJV).

It means then that the end goal of Christianity on the earth is to do what Jesus did and even greater works. Have we achieved that goal in our personal lives? No, we haven't.

There are doctrines that say the supernatural was for that time. Lies! That scripture was for all times, for all ages, and for all believers. The very least of those who believe in Jesus were able to do great things. Look at Stephen. He was chosen as a deacon.

Yet scripture says he operated in power. When was the last time you saw a deacon doing what Jesus did?

We are the temple of God. There is a paradox here where the temple is complete, but it is still being built. When we succeed in building a tabernacle for God to dwell, the supernatural becomes natural. But who are we that we can provide a dwelling place for the God of all creation, God of the angel-armies, God of all spirits? David asked the same question and answered it at the same time:

What is man that You are mindful of him, and the son of man that You visit him? For You have made him a little lower than the angels, and You have crowned him with glory and honor. You have made him to have dominion over the works of Your hands; You have put all things under his feet, all sheep and oxen—Even the beasts of the field, the birds of the air, and the fish of the sea that pass through the paths of the seas. (Psalm 8:4-8 - NKJV).

Here we see a description of man that mirrors original intent, yet this is not seemingly our reality—at least not yet. This same sentiment is echoed in Hebrews 2. The idea here is that redemption has a goal that is more than just getting salvation—it is about spiritual transformation from who we are now, or better yet, who we think we are now to who we were created to be.

Inclusively, if you are saved, you are saved. On the other hand, if you are saved and you want to change the world, you must first be transformed. Even Jesus had to go through the process of spiritual formation.

As we examine scripture, we see the 120, then the 70, then the 12, the 3, and finally the 1 (the disciple whom Jesus loved). All members are important, but who changed the world? Who shared the grandest of spiritual experiences? I am convinced that if we saw John today as he was then, we would think he was out of his mind.

Man was created a particular way to function a particular way before there was a fall. We will examine Job 38-39 to get a glimpse into what this may look like later. The mature son is able to absorb at least some of the responsibilities outlined in those chapters. Sonship is about responsibility. As you increase in maturity, there is also an increase in responsibilities. Imagine having to choose whether a hurricane hits a nation or not, knowing there may be casualties both ways.

There are spiritual dimensions we are not familiar with. Even our capacity to dream has been trivialized to our own detriment. Paul says we are to **"walk in the Spirit" (see Galatians 5:16).** This is not a metaphor. I once asked a pastor what it means, and he said to read your Bible, pray, fast, fellowship with the saints, and pretty much everything we do at "church." To walk in the spirit is to transcend physicality and actually, consciously traverse that realm. It is our capacity to go beyond the body. This phenomenon is called an "out of body" experience. There is no Biblical writer who wrote about spiritual things who did not know how to do this. The believer who desires more must begin to explore the spiritual dimensions.

Every author of the Bible knew what they were writing about. They were having real experiences outside the physical realm, though there is no language that can adequately capture what is experienced there. The consensus is, you really cannot tell it; one must experience it for themselves. Scripture then becomes this multi-dimensional gateway that cannot simply be interpreted in a natural sense. It must be understood from the perspective of Spirit.

- David says, **"Yea though I walk through the valley of the shadow of death." (see Psalm 23:4).**

- He says, **"Surely goodness and mercy shall follow me." (see Psalm 23:6).**

- He says, **"He who dwells in the secret place of the Most High shall abide under the shadow of the almighty." (see Psalm 91:1).**

These are all real places and real beings outside the physical world. Look at the experiences of Ezekiel and all the other prophets; examine John's experiences and visions. They all saw beyond this world as we need to learn to do as well. Until we can see beyond, our doctrine and interpretation of reality is really nothing but a guessing game. There is little to no wisdom in our interpretations without experience.

The Bible speaks about wisdom being present when God created the world (see Proverbs 8:1-4).

In this book, I want to have a candid conversation, and I hope you will bear with me. My times of theological studies are saturated with many questions and not all the answers. I have studied mystical theology for many years. I am also in the process of completing my master's in theology. So, truthfully, I have had the privilege of receiving the best of both worlds. With this book, I hope to create an acceptable bridge between both. The one question I know serious believers ask is, *"How can I tap into this supernatural reality so I can bring healing to the sick and deliverance to the oppressed?"* It is not only about saying the name of Jesus. Most believers are not willing to pay the price to walk in a certain level of spirituality, but every believer must have some measure of spirituality.

The Holy Spirit is in all of us, so there is a voice that speaks. I once asked my mentor for advice for a "non-mystic" Christian, and he said quite succinctly that there is no such thing as a non-mystic Christian. I now know this to be true. The definition of a mystic, according to the online dictionary, is:

> *a person who seeks by contemplation and self-surrender to obtain unity with or absorption into the Deity or the absolute, or who believes in the spiritual apprehension of truths that are beyond the intellect:*

Any believer who pursues the heart of God is a mystic. There are established laws that govern such a pursuit, and one of those laws is "stillness." Unless you learn to be still, you can never know God. This voice in all believers speaks and is rarely silent. Most of us ignore, doubt, or dismiss this voice. For those of us who listen, we experience different levels of manifestation and even prophetic insight. The challenge for us is to know this voice differently from all other voices. This comes with practice, trial and error. Practice in a safe environment. We cannot completely ignore voice, especially if we don't have spiritual sight. This small, still voice helped me shape the life I now live.

God made us highly intelligent beings. Ignorance is a choice. We may think we are not spiritual enough because we are not having the same experiences we read in the Bible, but it comes with growth and maturity. It means then that many who claim maturity due to their years of service to a church or years of being saved are really still babes in Christ. The one who is guided by that inner voice will grow spiritually. Here are some pointers:

- We must be willing to go where God wants to take us.

- We must not limit or doubt the kind of spiritual experiences we can have.

- Put no limits on God, so there are no limits on you.

- Be teachable. There is a lot you don't know. Don't be too quick to dismiss what others may say because you don't believe or it is contrary to your own beliefs.

- Study hard. Study always.

- Examine everything so you don't run the risk of missing God.

- Don't compare yourself to others. Embrace your own personal journey with the Lord.

- A still, small voice is as much God as an audible booming voice.

- Don't get stuck.

As we progress through this—I call it study—we will see who we were at the beginning, so we will have an idea of where we are going. God assumes the responsibility to get us there once we learn not to resist Him. We know we are located and positioned in His name, so it means we have access to the very depths of God and all spiritual and physical dimensions. After all, where Jesus is, we are also there. As He is, so are we. These are divine, unchangeable truths spoken to and about human beings who would step into the fullness of what God desires for them.

Let us not assume we know everything. Let us not assume we know God when we have never experienced Him or when we truly don't even know ourselves.

The expectation is that not all believers will become initiated sons, but all are children of the most high God. Enoch stood as an intercessor between God and fallen angels to the point where God had to firmly silence him on a matter. We see this also in the canon with Moses. This speaks to a Father-son relationship we have yet to experience. Only those initiated at this level of relationship with God can change the world.

All children go to heaven, but only sons have dominion and rule over the Father's estate. We are indeed gods on the earth. We are sons of God. You are a god to God—His offspring—in the same way you are a king and a priest to God, not to people. The standard set from the days of the law was that priests first minister to God before ministering to people. The priest would go into the holy of holies, then come out and engage with the people. It means as kings, priests, and gods, whatever we do in the form of ministry must flow out of our interaction and engagement with the presence of the living God.

We are on a journey. Salvation is not a destination. Going to heaven is not the ultimate goal of salvation.

Let's talk!

Read this book with a Bible nearby. Biblical references are made but not always quoted.

Chapter 1

LOVE BEYOND

Being called into the mystical/spiritual arena of Christianity is no walk in the park. People generally think we choose this path for ourselves, yet the hostility and indifference we face daily, plus the demands on the call and the protocols in place for walking in this realm is enough to make us wish we were normal like everyone else. It is not a path anyone truly desires to walk willingly because the price is high.

There is a very powerful and revealing verse of Scripture that can be used to form the foundation for this study. It speaks about the three most powerful things in this world:

And now abide faith, hope, love, these three; but the greatest of these is love. (1 Corinthians 13:13 - NKJV).

The Bible speaks about a great shaking in Hebrews 12:27:

Now this, "Yet once more," indicates the removal of those things that are being shaken, as of things that are made, that the things which cannot be shaken may remain. (NKJV).

There are two things that exist in creation: that which was created and established by God and that which was created and established by man. The devil doesn't create; he just manipulates. The great shaking is a prophetic utterance that there will come a day when everything will be shaken, and that which is not eternal will be removed, leaving behind only that which is eternal. Faith, Hope and Love will remain when all else is lost. So will you because we are eternal beings. Once we come into existence, we can never cease to exist. Faith, hope and love remains when all else is shaken because you remain. Apostle Paul also cites that Love is the greatest of the three. Why? We know that love sits at the very foundation of creation. God established this world, and all created worlds, on a foundation of Love because that is who He is. It means the absence of this very vital technology in our society is at the root of all ills. Iniquity increases where love is absent.

There are two things that bring a society to utter destruction: the absence of love and/or misdirected love. For example,

---

For the love of money is a root of all kinds of evil, for which some have strayed from the faith in their greediness, and pierced themselves through with many sorrows. (1 Timothy 6:10 – NKJV).

So, love directed at the wrong thing is equally as destructive as its absence.

The greatest call on the believer's life is to love. It is also the greatest challenge, for it doesn't come naturally for fallen beings. The death of the soul because of sin has caused us to grow calloused and self-serving. There is nothing wrong with loving our true self as God designed us, but a love of our false self is destructive.

A lot has been said so far, and I doubt I can unpack it all, but as you go through this study, I believe God will reveal even greater mysteries to you if you open your heart to Him.

If love is at the foundation of the world, then we should see it present throughout scripture. This is where we officially begin this study.

Then God said, "Let Us make man in Our image, according to Our likeness; let them have dominion over the fish of the sea, over the birds of the air, and over the cattle, over all the earth and over every creeping thing that creeps on the earth." (Genesis 1:26 – NKJV).

When the Godhead made a conscious decision to create man, love was perfected. God not only manifested Himself in creation as a creature, but He also established who He is intrinsically—Love. The Father created a son, who became the object and focus of His love. Humanity would soon become the greatest test of God's intrinsic capacity to love. History has taught us that loving someone who is perfect is easy. It takes little to no effort. The true test of our capacity to love is when we are called upon to love that which is not perfect.

If God didn't give His life for fallen humanity, He would not be Love. He would undoubtedly be something else. This is why marriages are so powerful because it tests our capacity to love that which is not perfect. While there are many exceptions, I'm sure, in many instances, the failure in marriage is a failure to truly love.

Adam and Eve were created perfect. They were a perfect manifestation of Love personified, but with the capacity to be something else—something not-God—by choice.

When Eve ate the fruit, she was no longer a living soul but a dead soul. Ezekiel 18:20 posits: **"The soul who sins shall die."** It was an immediate death that instantly changed Eve's physiology as a divine being created in the image and likeness of God. She changed. She died. Adam saw this happen right before his eyes. Now he had a choice to make. He could remain in his perfect, unfallen state and allow his wife —bone of his bone and flesh of his flesh—to die alone and face the consequences of her choice alone. I believe Adam's choice to disobey God was influenced by his love for his spouse. He chose death over eternal perfection and bliss. If Adam, as God's creation, could make such a choice fuelled by love, how could God, who is the epitome of Love, the one who personifies the very nature of Love, make a lesser choice? Adam's choice was not redemptive but plunged humanity into a fallen state. God's choice to die for humanity was redemptive and led to the restoration of Original Intent. We will talk about that later.

When man fell, Love was no longer the only force in existence. Something else came into our context. Whatever that was pushed a brother to commit murder. The taking of a human life by someone who cannot create life is the ultimate act of a reality that is not-God. This was not an act of love but something quite contrary…something God did not create or intend to establish in creation…something that came into existence by an act of will of a god-like being. This force is still at work in our world today, and the only thing in existence that can assuage the full blunt of this ungodly force is Love.

As I wrote this chapter, a lone Caucasian man went on a killing spree in the state of Maine. Eighteen people were murdered, and many more injured by this lone gunman. Days later, he was found dead from a self-inflicted gunshot wound. The absence of love creates a space for death. We may never know his story or the true motive behind this dastardly act, but we do know that whatever force drove him to act was not-God.

Most believers don't have the mental faculty to walk in certain spiritual realms. The call to love is a perfect example. The prophet Hosea was commanded by God to marry a prostitute. It is one of my all-time favourite Bible stories because of the depth of the message embedded in Hosea's obedience. Here is a man of God who is deeply challenged to love a woman who is as flawed as they can get. Yet his love is not at a level where she is constantly reminded of her flaws and how terrible she is, but Hosea learns to love her beyond her flaws to the point where her sins did not exist for him. This is the highest level of love that a human being can achieve. This is the God-kind of love.

I know very few people who can love others beyond their flaws. Most of us think it is our duty to point out people's flaws and call them out on their sins, but God requires more from us. I often wonder how He does it. He sees everything we do, yet His love for us is perfect. He doesn't even remind us of our sins and treat us according to our flaws. This is what perfect love looks like.

He has not dealt with us according to our sins, nor punished us according to our iniquities. (Psalm 103:10 - NKJV).

God doesn't punish sin as our doctrine has dictated for centuries. Sin creates its own consequences and punishment that we ourselves must bear fully unless God intervenes. Thank God He intervenes sometimes, because we truly cannot bear the full consequence of the sins we commit.

He has not dealt with us after our sins nor rewarded us according to our iniquities. For as the heavens are high above the earth, so great are His mercy and loving-kindness toward those who reverently and worshipfully fear Him. As far as the east is from the west, so far has He removed our transgressions from us. As a father loves and pities his children, so the Lord loves and pities those who fear Him [with reverence, worship, and awe]. For He knows our frame, He [earnestly] remembers and imprints [on His heart] that we are dust. (Psalm 103:10-14 - AMPC).

Can we love as God loves? It is impossible without God. The mental fortitude needed to love at this level must be developed through much practice and our willingness to submit to God.

Such hope never disappoints or deludes or shames us, for God's love has been poured out in our hearts through the Holy Spirit Who has been given to us. (Romans 5:5 - AMPC).

As a son of God, He orchestrates the experiences we need to love as He loves. He provides or allows the people and experiences in our lives to manifest that which we already possess. It is the higher call of the believer that many never attain to. Some may even think it is impossible, which is true. But God specializes in the impossible. There is nothing godly about calling out people's sins, as some take pleasure in doing. If it was you, you would not want that. Love covers a multitude of sins.

Above all things have intense and unfailing love for one another, for love covers a multitude of sins [forgives and disregards the offenses of others]. (1 Peter 4:8 - NKJV).

I have learned a valuable lesson on this mystical journey God has taken me on. We don't necessarily need to have the same experiences as Paul, Peter, Elijah, Ezekiel or even Enoch—though I still desire to have them. We know the experiences are all possible for us, but many of us have never seen an angel, heard the audible voice of God, experience an out-of-body encounter, or even seen a supernatural miracle, but if we learn to love beyond, we can change the world. God is perfectly God in the one who becomes love, and such a one will manifest the very essence and nature of who God is. Love is the very substance that established and manifested creation in the beginning so, it must also be perfected in us for there to be a new heaven and a new earth. *(Ooops. Now I've said too much!)*.

Let's see the conclusion of the matter in the words of our Master Himself:

"I am the true vine, and My Father is the vinedresser. Every branch in Me that does not bear fruit He takes away; and every branch that bears fruit He prunes, that it may bear more fruit. You are already clean because of the word which I have spoken to you. Abide in Me, and I in you. As the branch cannot bear fruit of itself, unless it abides in the vine, neither can you, unless you abide in Me. "I am the vine, you are the branches. He who abides in Me, and I in him, bears

much fruit; for without Me you can do nothing. If anyone does not abide in Me, he is cast out as a branch and is withered; and they gather them and throw them into the fire, and they are burned. If you abide in Me, and My words abide in you, you will ask what you desire, and it shall be done for you. By this My Father is glorified, that you bear much fruit; so you will be My disciples. "As the Father loved Me, I also have loved you; abide in My love. If you keep My commandments, you will abide in My love, just as I have kept My Father's commandments and abide in His love. "These things I have spoken to you, that My joy may remain in you, and that your joy may be full. This is My commandment, <u>that you love one another as I have loved you</u>. Greater love has no one than this, than to lay down one's life for his friends. You are My friends if you do whatever I command you. No longer do I call you servants, for a servant does not know what his master is doing; but I have called you friends, for all things that I heard from My Father I have made known to you. You did not choose Me, but I chose you and appointed you that you should go and bear fruit, and that your fruit should remain, that whatever you ask the Father in My name He may give you. These things I command you, that you love one another. (John 15:1-17 – NKJV).

Don't miss that. We demonstrate our love for God by loving each other. That is the command that Jesus is referring to when He said, **"If you love Me, keep my commandments."** It is not 613 commands, but two:

Jesus said to him, "'You shall love the Lord your God with all your heart, with all your soul, and with all your mind.'

This is the first and great commandment. And the second is like it: 'You shall love your neighbor as yourself.' (Matthew 22:37-39 - NKJV).

It is impossible to fulfil the first and great commandment without fulfilling the second, which means that in fulfilling the second commandment, we automatically fulfil the first. So, there is only one command: **Love one another.** These three words are the summative principle of God's interaction and engagement with humanity from the beginning until now. If the fulfilment of God's heart's desire for humanity could have been accomplished by just creating Adam, He would not have chosen to give Adam someone to love. It means then that the perfection of Love is not necessarily directed towards our Father, but to one another. We fulfil or perfect our love for God by loving one another.

Beloved, let us love one another, for love is of God; and everyone who loves is born of God and knows God. He who does not love does not know God, for God is love. In this the love of God was manifested toward us, that God has sent His only begotten Son into the world, that we might live through Him. In this is love, not that we loved God, but that He loved us and sent His Son to be the propitiation for our sins. Beloved, if God so loved us, we also ought to love one another. (1 John 4:7-11 - NKJV).

No one has seen God at any time. If we love one another, God abides in us, and His love has been perfected in us. By this we know that we abide in Him, and He in us, because He has given us of His Spirit. And we have seen and testify that the Father has sent the Son as Savior of the world. Whoever confesses that Jesus is the Son of God, God abides in him, and

41

he in God. And we have known and believed the love that God has for us. God is love, and he who abides in love abides in God, and God in him. (1 John 4:12-16 - NKJV).

Love has been perfected among us in this: that we may have boldness in the day of judgment; because as He is, so are we in this world. There is no fear in love; but perfect love casts out fear, because fear involves torment. But he who fears has not been made perfect in love. We love Him because He first loved us. (1 John 4:17-19 - NKJV).

If someone says, "I love God," and hates his brother, he is a liar; for he who does not love his brother whom he has seen, how can he love God whom he has not seen? And this commandment we have from Him: that he who loves God must love his brother also. (1 John 4:20-21 - NKJV).

God directs our love to one another because He wants us to see Himself in others. Human beings make poor choices. We make bad, deadly, stupid, selfish, and rebellious decisions, sometimes without considering the possible consequences. Still, we are all God's prized creation, and God loves humanity enough to give His life, even for those He knows would reject Him. This is love. We cannot hate, despise, judge, condemn, gossip, tear down, cheat, deceive, manipulate, and enslave one another, then claim to love God.

But what does this kind of love really look like? Apostle Paul tells us:

Though I speak with the tongues of men and of angels, but have not love, I have become sounding brass or a clanging

cymbal. And though I have the gift of prophecy, and understand all mysteries and all knowledge, and though I have all faith, so that I could remove mountains, but have not love, I am nothing. And though I bestow all my goods to feed the poor, and though I give my body to be burned, but have not love, it profits me nothing. Love suffers long and is kind; love does not envy; love does not parade itself, is not puffed up; does not behave rudely, does not seek its own, is not provoked, thinks no evil; does not rejoice in iniquity, but rejoices in the truth; bears all things, believes all things, hopes all things, endures all things. Love never fails. But whether there are prophecies, they will fail; whether there are tongues, they will cease; whether there is knowledge, it will vanish away. For we know in part and we prophesy in part. But when that which is perfect has come, then that which is in part will be done away. When I was a child, I spoke as a child, I understood as a child, I thought as a child; but when I became a man, I put away childish things. For now we see in a mirror, dimly, but then face to face. Now I know in part, but then I shall know just as I also am known. And now abide faith, hope, love, these three; but the greatest of these is love. (1 Corinthians 13:1-13 - NKJV).

In case you missed it, let me itemize them for you:

1. Love suffers long and is kind
2. Love does not envy
3. Love does not parade itself and is not puffed up
4. Love does not behave itself rudely
5. Love does not seek its own
6. Love is not provoked

7. Love thinks no evil
8. Love does not rejoice in iniquity
9. Love rejoices in the truth
10. Love bears all things
11. Love believes all things
12. Love hopes all things
13. Love endures all things
14. Love never fails.

Was Paul a trusted authority on this subject? Well, we are talking about the man who was zealous for his Judaic beliefs that he heavily persecuted the Christian church until God called him to become one of the very people he persecuted. I imagine that was no easy feat for a man like this to approach the church saying he is now one of them. In today's world, we would assume he was working undercover to further his dastardly agenda.

Love suffers long and is kind...

One question I have been asked, does one stay in an abusive marriage? My personal answer is no, run for your life. But, from another perspective, the one who does commands the attention of heaven if that decision is fuelled by love and hope. Many abusive marriages have turned into something quite the opposite because of love. Many have not.

Love does not envy...

Do we celebrate each other's wins? Are we happy for the people who achieve the very things we only dream about? Or do we always want to be ahead of everyone else, and in our hearts, we cannot be happy for people who have what we want?

Love does not parade itself and is not puffed up…

Many people getting married create a great spectacle of their wedding to impress other people. This is not necessarily an act of love. There is no pride in love. We often do things in the name of love and we want the world to know. We want to be acknowledged and praised for what we do. This is not love. It is a selfish pursuit of grandeur.

Love does not behave itself rudely…

Love does not seek its own…

Love is always other-centered. It doesn't seek validation or praise, just fulfilment. Love gives, expecting nothing in return.

Love is not (easily) provoked…

Love thinks no evil…

Are you always focusing on people's faults? Do you think of hurting people who have hurt you? Do you imagine that driver who almost ran you off the road would meet an unfortunate demise further down the road?

Love does not rejoice in iniquity…

Do you feel good when others have fallen? Do you have that little jittery feeling in your stomach when relaying someone's faults to others?

Love rejoices in the truth…

Love bears all things…

Love believes all things…

We can even think of Mary as a young unmarried woman with child, and her husband-to-be who was asked in a dream to believe that she had not committed any sin to be with a child. Who in our world today would believe such a thing? We buy lotto numbers from dreams, not receive divine messages from the other world.

Love hopes all things…

Love endures all things…

Love never fails…

Maybe you are in a difficult marriage with an unfaithful spouse, or you have difficult children who have forgotten what you tried to teach them growing up. Maybe you are in a stressful and demanding job with a narcissistic boss or life for you is just plain difficult; consider these things the training ground for you to learn to love beyond.

Study this chapter until you know it by heart because herein lies the secret to a new heaven and a new earth. You may have to give your life for this love to manifest fully in this world, but…

Greater love has no one than this, than to lay down one's life for his friends. (John 15:13 - NKJV).

Chapter 2

ORIGINAL INTENT

If all scripture is inspired, and not one jot or tittle is wasted, then we must look at every verse, even the ones we want to ignore. We cannot approach the Bible selectively but look at scripture (even the books that did not make the canon) as a whole. This knowledge prompted me to always go back to the beginning; our starting point. The key to humanity's true form is embedded in the mind of God when He said, **"Let us make man…"**

As you approach the book of Genesis, particularly the first three chapters, several questions arise:

1. Who is God?

2. If God is light, why did He have to create light to dissipate darkness?

3. How is there day and night without the sun and moon?

4. Who is the "us" God is referring to in Genesis 1:26?

5. Why wasn't the likeness mentioned in Genesis 1:27?

6. What happened on Day 2? Why was it the only day God did not see or say it was good?

I don't have the answers to all these questions, but I have probed some of them. When God created man, He spoke the purpose, so that is no secret:

Then God said, "Let Us make man in Our image, according to Our likeness; let them have dominion over the fish of the sea, over the birds of the air, and over the cattle, over all the earth and over every creeping thing that creeps on the earth." (Genesis 1:26 - NKJV).

The man we know today is not operating at that level. We are afraid of lizards, cockroaches, heights, death, the unknown, and a long list of fears and phobias. We have not experienced walking out the purpose that God spoke in the beginning because of the fall. We know ourselves based on the context of the fall, even those who are sweetly saved.

Then God blessed them, and God said to them, "Be fruitful and multiply; fill the earth and subdue it; have dominion over the fish of the sea, over the birds of the air, and over every living thing that moves on the earth." (Genesis 1:28 - NKJV).

Has the mandate changed? I do not believe it has.

And God said, "See, I have given you every herb that yields seed which is on the face of all the earth, and every tree whose fruit yields seed; to you it shall be for food." (Genesis 1:29 - NKJV).

There goes the secret to divine health that went out the window now for generations with the advent of processed and fast foods. Embedded in these three verses is what we will call "Original Intent." This is what we lost when we fell. You could call this the original nature of the kingdom of which we were made to rule and govern as a son of God.

Note here that God created a full-grown man and woman. He created sons who were able to have children (maybe not the way we do post-fall) and raise them up as sons. Salvation is not an automatic initiation into sonship. *A child is born; a son is given. We* are born again or born from above as children, but must matriculate into sonship. This is not an automatic initiation due to years of service to the church or being a long-standing member.

For though by this time you ought to be teachers, you need someone to teach you again the first principles of the oracles of God; and you have come to need milk and not solid food. For everyone who partakes only of milk is unskilled in the word of righteousness, for he is a babe. But solid food belongs to those who are of full age, that is, those who by reason of use have their senses exercised to discern both good and evil. (Hebrews 5:12-14 - NKJV).

You can be in church for decades and serve on every committee imaginable and still be a child.

If the original mandate remains unchanged, then the path of salvation is trying to get us back to that, where the end becomes the beginning.

There was a fall in Genesis 3 that resulted in a change in how man functioned and his relationship to the divine. Redemption is supposed to take us back to that place of relational bliss with God, where His power and authority over all things flow through us unhindered. Paul says something very interesting:

Behold what manner of love the Father has bestowed on us, that we should be called children of God! Therefore the world does not know us, because it did not know Him. Beloved, now we are children of God; and it has not yet been revealed what we shall be, but we know that when He is revealed, we shall be like Him, for we shall see Him as He is. (1 John 3:1-2 - NKJV).

So the full manifestation of who we are is hidden from our knowledge. Why? Is this a classic case of not being able to handle the truth?

Moses saw creation as it unfolded. He must have seen man is his glorious estate. Maybe this is why he cared so much for the rebellious people because he saw their true form. Moses was also one of the two who met Jesus on the mount of transfiguration. Wait! Wasn't he dead? The Bible literally says those who are in Christ do not die, and even if they do, God raises them up. We will talk more about that later.

Jesus said to her, "I am the resurrection and the life. He who believes in Me, though he may die, he shall live. And whoever lives and believes in Me shall never die. Do you believe this?" (John 11:25-26 - NKJV).

The bones of Elisha brought a dead man to life. How was this even possible? The conclusion here is that scripture records many things we know nothing about. But instead of admitting this, we pretend to know or just ignore certain scriptures altogether. Every believer must decide for themselves if we serve a God who can do the impossible or not.

Who is God?

The Bible did not give us an autobiography or a personal introduction to God. It just says, "In the beginning, God..." There was or could not be a formal introduction because God has always been. We know Him as the self-existing one, which means, He is the no-thing before there was something, and He is everything. It means the revelation we see in scripture about God is in relation to humanity.

God establishes creation, then creates someone like Him to govern it. We could say the human being is God creating a perfect replica of Himself in a physical space. Why else would the language say, "In His likeness and image." It means there are similarities that would be indistinguishable to anyone standing on the outside looking in.

There are those who believe that there are several creations between Genesis 1 and 5. This may or may not be true, but from our viewpoint, we could say the Adam in Genesis 1 (made in the image and likeness) is different from the Adam in Genesis 2 (made a living soul), different from Adam in Genesis 5 (made in the likeness of God). But let's keep the discussion simple. Man was made in the image of God. An image of something is an almost perfect replica of the thing being imaged. Just think of yourself looking in the mirror. There is an image looking back, which is you, but we know who the real you is.

We know who the real God is. We were made a replica; an image looking back at Him. So when God looks at us, He should see Himself.

Image is also a derivative of imagination, which suggests that when God made man, He established what He, God, imagined Himself to look like if He was a physical being.

So we see the image, but where is the likeness?

Some say the image is created or formed, but the likeness is achieved through relationship.

We can look at the temptation in Genesis 3:4-5.

Then the serpent said to the woman, "You will not surely die. For God knows that in the day you eat of it your eyes will be opened, and you will be like God, knowing good and evil."

Eve's temptation was to be "like God." How do we quantify this with the discussion we are having about being sons of God? Remember, satan didn't fall because he wanted to be like God. He wanted to BE God. There is a difference. Angels were not created to "be like God" or to "be God" but to minister to those who are like Him.

No one can dethrone or replace God. It is literally impossible, and to think in such a way is suicide. Ask King Herod and those like him. Their declaration was not that they were "like God";

they said they WERE GOD. Let's keep things in proper perspective.

It is quite possible that the likeness is missing from Genesis 1:27 because it was not yet achieved. If this is correct, then man fell before achieving likeness. We could also say they wanted to jump ahead of God or achieve something that should be done within the context of a relationship, without the relationship. This can be likened to those of us who have no relationship with God but want His power to flow through us. We want the benefits but not the Benefactor.

If God became man, and man fell, it means man is somehow a fallen version of God. God has not fallen, but the man in God has fallen. God has not sinned, but man in God has sinned.

The fullness of the redeemed and transformed, transfigured immortal God-man is not the sum total of who God is. God made Himself as man, but man does not represent the fullness of who God is. I don't even think this is possible. We know God as God has revealed Himself, and in our context, He has revealed Himself to and in humanity. The Bible then is a narrative that reveals God becoming a physical being, that being falling, and the rise and redemption of that being by virtue of the Son of God, who is the sum-total of all humanity was meant to be.

Love has been perfected among us in this: that we may have boldness in the day of judgment; because as He is, so are we in this world. (1 John 4:17 - NKJV).

Personally, I would not believe any of this is true if it was not written in Scripture.

Let's dig a little deeper.

This is the history of the heavens and the earth when they were created, in the day that the Lord God made the earth and the heavens, before any plant of the field was in the earth and before any herb of the field had grown. For the Lord God had not caused it to rain on the earth, and there was no man to till the ground; (Genesis 2:4-5 - NKJV).

Notice the language "in the day" not "days." Are we looking at a new creation here? Genesis 2 reveals man as a living soul. His body was formed by God, and God breathed into his nostrils, and he became a living soul. This is different from the "male and female created He them" in Genesis 1. I know what "sound doctrine" teaches about these verses, but if we were studying this at the University level, we would not draw the same conclusions. It is almost as if we are afraid to believe anything different from what the masses believe.

Let us note three things from the above text:

1. No plants
2. No herbs of the field
3. No rain
4. No man

As we continue reading, we are introduced to a living being or a living soul. God plants a garden towards the east of Eden and places the man there. Two points to note:

1. East is a direction we will see come up several times in Scripture. For example, the Wise Men came from the east.

2. Eden is a location with a garden in it. So Eden is not just a garden. When the Bible says the Garden of Eden, it's speaking about the garden in Eden.

The living soul (man) is placed in the garden. According to Greek and Hebrew, Eden can be interpreted as "paradise." We see this word being used in Luke 23:43:

And Jesus said to him, "Assuredly, I say to you, today you will be with Me in Paradise."

Eden, by definition, is a pristine place of abundant natural beauty; a place of delight and pleasure. Remember, God created the heavens (always plural) and the earth. So we cannot interpret Bible as if it is only referring to the earth and places on earth.

Here is a possibility; Eden may not be a place on earth but in the heavens. As a matter of fact, earth is also in the heavens. The earth is floating in space.

A river flows out of Eden to water the garden; from there, it divides into four rivers. Before the river, there are two specific trees inside the garden:

1. Tree of life
2. Tree of the knowledge of good and evil.

The river parts four ways:

1. Pison, in the land of Havilah (gold). Pison is mentioned only once in scripture. Havilah seems to be a place and also the name of a person.

2. Gihon is a place referenced in 1 Kings and 2 Chronicles. It compasseth the land of Ethiopia.

3. Hiddekel is mentioned in Daniel 10:4 – East of Assyria.

4. Euphrates is mentioned over nineteen times in Scripture. A study of these references will reveal that Euphrates is usually linked to some spiritual experiences.

A couple of years ago, I had a revelation to look into the possibility that Eden is also in the heart of man. This is how my journey began into seeing reality from a multi-dimensional view and not just from one purview.

When we get saved, we ask Jesus to come into our hearts. In my research, I realized that the heart had four chambers for the flow of blood. Coincidence? I digged deeper. I looked at the spiritual meaning of the names of each of the rivers. I found some awesome revelations there, but this is not the book for that.

If God lives in you, then there is a throne in you. The river flows from the throne. This is how I began to understand two scriptures:

Keep your heart with all diligence, for out of it spring the issues of life. (Proverbs 4:23 - NKJV).

He who believes in Me, as the Scripture has said, out of his heart will flow rivers of living water. (John 7:38 - NKJV).

Coincidence? Not very likely. Out of the heart of man flows a river that shapes our reality. This is why maintaining pure thoughts is imperative for the believer because impure thoughts will muddy the waters and cause you to experience a reality you do not want.

Water is one of the elemental dimensions that a son learns to master:

1. Moses parting the Red Sea.
2. Turning water to blood.
3. Bringing water from a rock.
4. Jesus walking on water.
5. Peter walking on water (a few steps is good enough for me).
6. Turning water to wine.
7. Parting the Jordan river.

Water also has a whole lot of significance to spirituality. That is why I believe baptism in water is so important. Even Moses and the Israelites passing through the Red Sea was considered a baptism.

And there are three that bear witness on earth: the Spirit, the water, and the blood; and these three agree as one. (1 John 5:8 - NKJV).

The man was put in the garden to cultivate and keep it. This is not what we know today because there were no tools; pipes, hoses, forks, rakes, etc. Sonship comes with accountability and responsibility. If we can scarcely bear the burden of mentorship, then we are not ready for that level of function. We have some growing up to do.

Man was given a command not to eat from the tree of the knowledge of good and evil. In the day he eats, he will surely die. God knew the man would eat, so why put the tree there in the first place? I don't believe the original sin had anything to do with sex, as some people teach, but sex is a good example to answer that question. Why do we have the capacity to want sex long before we are ready for marriage? The sex is there to have from the moment you start wanting it, but it is forbidden until a certain appointed time. To partake before that time has consequences.

So there was a time for the man and woman to partake of that tree, but the time was not yet. The keywords in that command are: *eat and knowledge.*

What kind of fruit does a tree of knowledge bear? Surely not an apple. To eat is to consume or ingest. Knowledge is to know; information. In other words, man was told not to consume any information relating to good and evil because he was not ready for that.

The best we can do as immature believers is to try our best to obey God.

There is no comparison between how we are now and how we functioned as a living soul before sin. The fall literally caused a devolution of man. We did not sweat, pee, vomit; as a matter of fact, we did not have skin as we have now.

So to eat from a tree is not eating as we know now. Let me give you an example:

> **In the meantime His disciples urged Him, saying, "Rabbi, eat." But He said to them, "I have food to eat of which you do not know." (John 4:31-32 - NKJV).**

All these scriptures are called by some great teachers of our day "Passover scriptures." We just read them and pass right over.

God says it is not good for man to be alone. He made him a help meet. This word "help" is the same root word used in Psalm when it speaks about God being our help. God put a deep sleep on Adam and brought forth the woman. She was named woman. Eve is a name given to her after the fall. Woman is not a derogatory term. It actually speaks to original intent. So when Jesus looked at Mary and called her "Woman," that was intentional.

The man and the woman were naked and not ashamed. What did nakedness look like for man who had no skin as we have now? We will address this and more in the next chapter.

Chapter 3

THE GARDEN OF EDEN

Son of man, take up a lamentation for the king of Tyre, and say to him, 'Thus says the Lord God: "You were the seal of perfection, full of wisdom and perfect in beauty. You were in Eden, the garden of God; every precious stone was your covering: the sardius, topaz, and diamond, beryl, onyx, and jasper, sapphire, turquoise, and emerald with gold. The workmanship of your timbrels and pipes was prepared for you on the day you were created. "You were the anointed cherub who covers; I established you; You were on the holy mountain of God; You walked back and forth in the midst of fiery stones. You were perfect in your ways from the day you were created, till iniquity was found in you. "By the abundance of your trading you became filled with violence within, and you sinned; therefore I cast you as a profane thing out of the mountain of God; and I destroyed you, O covering cherub, from the midst of the fiery stones." (Ezekiel 28:12-16 - NKJV).

We know from this text that Eden is the Garden of God, and God planted a garden in Eden where He put man. The question is, was Eden on earth? I believe earth became a focal point for man after the fall because he no longer had access to the heavens. Remember, God created the heavens and the earth in the beginning before He created man as a living soul. So, man had access to both the earth and the heavens. There are theologians who believe the fall was actually from a higher reality to a lower more confined one.

What we want to do as we continue this discussion is to think of man's existence from both the heavens (hashamayim) and the earth. What did we lose when we fell? We must have lost something. Why is it so difficult for us to see beyond our earthly perception?

The Garden of God was not destroyed by the fall, but man was put outside.

Eden appears twenty times in Scripture. We also see the derivative word *Paradise* four times, depending on which translation you are looking at. A word study on any of these words will yield some great mystery. My conclusion from study is that what is above is reflected below. So the Garden of God existed above, and there was a counterpart that was below. Earth is a reflection of heaven. Why else would Jesus tell us to pray: **"On earth as it is in heaven." (See Matthew 6:10. Luke 11:2).**

It is not in heaven as it is on earth. So man has, even to this day, a pivotal role in the nurturing of the earth. What we see happening today is pollution and a total disregard for the earth because we think it is going to be destroyed. What if the plan of God is transmutation and not destruction? Wouldn't we have a role to play in that as well? There is a disregard for some of the simplest things that would contribute to nurturing the earth, for example, planting trees, growing our own food, and not littering.

When discussing Eden, the mystery is knowing which Eden is being referenced in a particular scripture.

The Garden of God still exists, and there is a cherub and a flaming sword at the entrance, but as a believer in Christ, we can walk right in. Here's the challenge: If all we see and believe is what we can interact with in the physical world, then it is going to be a challenge to fathom the spiritual dimensions (plural). Man in his original state was not like the man we know as ourselves today, but more like the man we will become in the future.

We try to relegate a lot of the heavenly places into an earthly perspective when we really just need to learn how to walk in the Spirit and develop our spiritual sight, which is really our "other eye." Yes, I see the religious red flags going up. Let me quote scripture:

the eyes of your understanding being enlightened; that you may know what is the hope of His calling, what are the riches of the glory of His inheritance in the saints. (Ephesians 1:18 - NKJV).

The lamp of the body is the eye. If therefore your eye is good, your whole body will be full of light. But if your eye is bad, your whole body will be full of darkness. If therefore the light that is in you is darkness, how great is that darkness! (Matthew 6:22-23 - NKJV).

Let's say it this way: If another eye exists in the makeup of humanity, then it must be God who put it there. The other eye is not demonic or evil; it is human. It is how you use that eye that determines its nature. My personal belief is that this eye or eyes are the eyes of the soul. It is our inbuilt capacity to see the other world, which we are born with. As children, we are able to see with even greater clarity the unseen world. So something happens as we grow that causes us to lose this ability. I think it may be linked to our pineal gland. It is a tiny endocrine gland in the middle of your brain that helps regulate your body's circadian rhythm by secreting the hormone melatonin. But it does more than that. Research has linked this gland to our capacity as a human being to interact with the world outside physicality. The pineal gland can be calcified, or in law man's term, hardened. Here is a fun fact: long-term fluoride use is known to cause the hardening of the pineal gland.

Here we begin to have an understanding of why we struggle to see. The eyes of the soul for most believers are darkened. We struggle to see the world beyond this physical one. Most believers today can't tell the difference between an angel and a demon. We must be careful about the level of conformity we have to the systems of this world because they are designed to suppress our spirituality so we can be controlled. I will say no more on that. There is a greater benefit to you, if you conduct your own research.

It is doubtless not profitable for me to boast. I will come to visions and revelations of the Lord: I know a man in Christ who fourteen years ago—whether in the body I do not know, or whether out of the body I do not know, God knows—such a one was caught up to the third heaven. And I know such a man—whether in the body or out of the body I do not know, God knows— how he was caught up into Paradise and heard

inexpressible words, which it is not lawful for a man to utter. (2 Corinthians 12:1-4 - NKJV).

The word *paradise* is also a reference to Eden, according to Biblical commentary. The Eden we see in Ezekiel 28:13 and Genesis 2:8 is in reference to Adam's home. Eden comes from the word *pleasure and delight,* which comes from the root word meaning to delight in self or live voluptuously. So man is put in the garden of God, where God experiences pleasure and delight in His creation. I imagine this was a beautiful experience for God, for He delighted in Himself because He was looking at a perfect replica of Himself in creation, and He saw that it was very good.

In Genesis 3, we see the fall of the God-made man. By one man, all humanity fell. Similarly, by one Man, all humanity is redeemed, but this redemption can only be accessed as an act of a man's will. Though redemption is available to all human beings, it can only be accessed by will. This conjures up a few questions:

1. **What constituted salvation for those who lived before Christ?**

We know faith played a role as Abraham believed God and it was appointed to him as righteousness. We also know many saints rose when Christ was crucified, so in a sense, their redemption was complete. We don't like to talk about it, but our belief that there is just one final resurrection in the future is a bit flawed because the Bible records several resurrections.

2. Are there ways to connect to God, have a relationship, and be saved without all the church stuff?

I believe Jesus Christ is our Lord and Saviour, and by Him, we are saved. I also believe there are other ways to access the spiritual world, though in a limited and illegal sense.

Most assuredly, I say to you, he who does not enter the sheepfold by the door, but climbs up some other way, the same is a thief and a robber. (John 10:1 - NKJV).

The reason people in the occult and any such sect are able to operate in some measure of power is because it speaks to human capacity, not demonic influence. A human being can walk on water, walk through walls, have out-of-body experiences, and everything supernatural we read in scripture because a human being can, not because they are empowered by the demonic.

Study the fall of man very carefully. Adam and Eve were not forced to disobey God. Their will was not overridden. They believed something suggested to them and acted on it, thereby losing their power and access. It is the same for us today. They were made in the image and likeness of God, so why was the likeness a temptation to them? Further on, we will talk about the likeness not yet achieved, but surely it was there, at the very least, potentially.

Another thing to note is that Christianity operates as a religion and is thereby restricted as a system of this world. This is why politics and such can easily align with the church for societal issues, even though they differ morally. I believe in untethering from all systems of the world to operate at the level we were made to operate. I have heard people say they want to effect change by operating within the system, but this is not possible because there will always be a demand for conformity. The true gospel will come under heavy persecution from the system of religion and from the world.

Paul says in Romans 12 that we should not conform to the systems of this world but be transformed by the renewing of the mind; thereby, we become agents of transformation to that very system we are no longer conformed to.

When man fell, a curse was pronounced. Who caused the fall of man? The serpent. What was revealed about the serpent suggests that it was the only one of its kind. Could it be that this creature existed only to cause the fall of man? The Bible continues to talk about fiery serpents, flying serpents, leviathan (the twisted serpent), but no direct scripture to say the serpent was satan, except Revelation 12:9.

I believe there are dimensions that only those inundated with the blood of Christ can access, and there are no satans there. It is remiss of us to think that fallen beings still have full access to places where God dwells, paradise being one of them.

This serpent, for some reason, had access to the Garden of God and was able to get close enough to the woman to have a conversation. The serpent told the woman that her eyes would be opened. Which eye? If one has access to both the heavens and the earth, what more was there to see? This suggestion of lack was unfounded.

Watch the progression to the fall:

1. She saw that the tree was good for food.

2. It was a delight to her eyes.

3. She desired the wisdom it would give her.

There are a few take-aways from this scenario:

1. **Sight and desire can lead to a fall.**

If you see and desire something you want, you will go for it.

2. **The belief that God is holding something back from you can lead to a fall.**

All things are yours, but that doesn't mean you can handle access to all things now. If you had a newborn baby and decided to buy a car so they don't have to struggle when they get to college, at what point will you hand over the keys? Yet, from the moment you buy the car, it belongs to them.

It is believed that the tree was always meant for them, but the timing was wrong.

What is even more interesting was that the woman ate, then gave to her husband, and he ate. There was no conversation. The serpent did not talk to Adam. It means then that as perfect as the man and woman were, free will made them susceptible to evil as is still the case for all humanity. You don't need to have a conversation with a devil or anyone to do the wrong thing.

So the eyes of both of them were opened. Which eyes were they using before? They knew they were naked; how were they clothed before? The most justifiable explanation I have heard so far is that as a living soul, the soul being the real you, the soul was on the outside, and the body was inside the soul. When man died, no longer a living soul, the soul went inside—the soul died.

I have had the strange experience of feeling my soul extending beyond my body. It means that man was such a glorious being, he had the potential to expand and contract, self-duplicate, go anywhere in the heavens or on the earth. Man was the governor of creation; there was no place he didn't have access to: physical or spiritual.

They heard God approaching. So, even in their fallen state, they had clarity of the spiritual dimensions. They went to hide among the trees in the garden. The language of scripture is interesting. They didn't hide behind but among. God is Spirit, and how He sees the world is different from us, unless He looks through our eyes. A spirit viewing the physical dimensions sees only waves of energetic structures. Adam and Eve would have looked no different from the trees at this point, so God asked, "Where are you?"

Ezekiel 31 is a good study on humanity as trees.

The Lord God seemingly could not identify man because he now appeared no different from the trees because he had fallen.

So, the man says:

1. He heard God.
2. He was afraid.
3. He was naked.
4. He hid.

God knew the man had fallen. This was a different response to God than what was the norm. The relational connection was severed, and man was walking a new and different path for the very first time.

God asked the man if he had disobeyed, to which the man replied, **"The woman whom You gave to be with me, she gave me from the tree, and I ate."** There was no conversation between the man and woman, but the man still blamed her for his dilemma.

A characteristic of the fall of humanity is our affinity to not accept responsibility for our actions. Fallen angels don't blame others for their bad decisions. So, the first thing sonship addresses is taking responsibility: **"I take responsibility for my sins, thereby I repent."**

The woman did the blame-game as well, **"The serpent deceived me, and I ate."** She was honest. God addressed the serpent first (see Genesis 3:14-15).

The serpent's curse was to eat dust all of its days. Man was made from dust. I believe this is one of the reasons we age and die. There is a serpentine nature that exists in man that feeds on the body. If we can kill the serpent, we will not see death.

"The wolf and the lamb shall feed together, the lion shall eat straw like the ox, and dust shall be the serpent's food. They shall not hurt nor destroy in all My holy mountain," Says the Lord. (Isaiah 65:25 - NKJV).

The hostility that occurs thereafter between the seed of the serpent and the seed of the woman is both internal and external. When the Bible says you are given authority to trample on serpents and scorpions and over all the power of the enemy, and nothing by any means can hurt you (see Luke 10:19), it is also speaking to the internal battles we must overcome. *The devils cannot really hurt you, but they can deceive you into hurting yourself.*

Everything you need to overcome to shine like the stars is embedded within you, not outside. Our greatest battles will be to overcome the traits embedded in our fallen bodies, those desires to over-indulge or partake of a *tree* before it is time.

After the fall, creation changed.

For the creation was subjected to futility, not willingly, but because of Him who subjected it in hope; because the creation itself also will be delivered from the bondage of corruption into the glorious liberty of the children of God. (Romans 8:20-21 - NKJV).

God had to suppress creation so it doesn't rule over fallen man, though in some sense, it still does. Human beings have many phobias, from the smallest of insects to our fear of heights. It speaks to how much our nature had changed as we now became earth-dwellers. Our capacity to move in the heavenly realms was dissolved.

Man must have looked so strange at this point, until God addressed that.

Also for Adam and his wife the Lord God made tunics of skin, and clothed them. (Genesis 3:21 - NKJV).

This has been interpreted as animal skin; that God killed an animal and clothed the man and woman. I have even heard that He did so with the blood still dripping from the skin as a symbol of what was to come. The Bible does not support this thought.

71

There are proper translation of this text that suggest that God made "garments of skin" or "coats of skin" to clothe man (see KJV, ASV).

It is at this point that God put skin on man, the skin we know now. Keep in mind that scriptural references to "garment" is not always a physical term, but it also has a spiritual connotation.

A human being has three layers of skin…some say seven, some say ten, but let's work with the three:

1. Epidermis – the outermost layer
2. Dermis – contains touch connective tissue, hair follicles, and sweat glands
3. Hypodermis

The second layer gives us the capacity to sweat, yet God said before clothing man with skin "By the sweat of your brows…" Man was unable to sweat before he was clothed with skin.

In the garden was a tree of life. This tree was the source of immortality. Even though man had fallen, if they had access to the tree, they would still have access to immortality. So God sent the man out of the Garden of Eden.

The cherub and flaming sword were put east of the garden of Eden to guard the way to the tree of life, not necessarily to prevent man from accessing Eden. Adam and Eve must have had children before the fall, but their first sons after the fall that we know about are Cain and Abel. When Cain committed murder, he left the presence of God and went to Nod, east of Eden.

Compare these two verses to see how close in proximity man was to Eden even after the fall:

So He drove out the man; and He placed cherubim at the east of the garden of Eden, and a flaming sword which turned every way, to guard the way to the tree of life. (Genesis 3:24 - NKJV).

Then Cain went out from the presence of the Lord and dwelt in the land of Nod on the east of Eden. (Genesis 4:16 - NKJV).

There are things we need to note as we approach the closing of this chapter:

1. Man still had access to the presence of God even after the fall.

2. Man heard the voice of God with clarity.

3. God still had a vested interest in the affairs and life of man.

What happened to man throughout history? How did we lose this clarity? Is it truly a matter of consciousness and awareness? Or are we just sleeping? If you try to have a conversation with someone who is sleeping, they will not hear you. Could it be God is still speaking, but we are sleeping while awake in the natural? If this is the case, then how do we wake up? If I suggest the need for spiritual enlightenment for every believer, you will call me new age. I don't mind, since my Lord and Saviour is God of all ages, new and old.

The tree of life is an interesting study as this is a technology the occultic people seem to use as well, though I imagine a more counterfeit version. We have access to the real thing. The tree of life also shows up throughout scripture, and it is there in Revelation.

Seeing scripture from a purely earthly perspective will limit our purview of what was and what is to come. We must study scripture from a multi-dimensional perspective in order to understand sonship. The Garden of Eden may not have been on earth because man was created to rule in the heavens (cosmos) and the earth.

For centuries, only scientists have shown an interest in what exists outside of the earth realm in the physical world. For the most part, believers think it is irrelevant to their existence, yet, the Bible says:

And He said to them, "Go into all the world and preach the gospel to every creature." (Mark 16:15 - NKJV).

Have you ever looked up the root word for "World?" Let me copy from the Strong's Accordance that we are all familiar with:

> 2889. kosmos
> **Original Word:** κόσμος, ου, ὁ
> **Transliteration:** kosmos
> **Phonetic Spelling:** (kos'-mos)
> **Definition:** order, the world
> **Usage:** the world, universe; worldly affairs; the inhabitants of the world; adornment.

Do you realize there is no scripture that says believers will die and go to heaven? What it does say is that we are seated with Christ in "heavenly places," which really gives us a more cosmic view of reality, our existence, and our purpose. As it was in the beginning, so shall it be in the end.

Chapter 4

THE POWER OF ONE

After the fall of man, I believe men continued to fall in their consciousness, until the earth was full of corruption.

God saw that human evil was out of control. People thought evil, imagined evil—evil, evil, evil from morning to night. God was sorry that he had made the human race in the first place; it broke his heart. God said, "I'll get rid of my ruined creation, make a clean sweep: people, animals, snakes and bugs, birds—the works. I'm sorry I made them." (Genesis 6:5-7 - MSG).

Essentially, when God decided to wipe out all living things, it would have brought the world back to what it was in Genesis 1:2: Void, darkness, the waters above not yet separated from the waters below. This would have been an almost complete reset of creation.

There was one man on earth who was untouched by the corruption, and by that one man, complete annihilation of the human race was averted.

But Noah was different. God liked what he saw in Noah. (Genesis 6:8 - MSG).

Noah was commissioned to build an ark. This was, by definition, a huge structure that, in our day, would require heavy machinery and manpower. If you research a similar process, you will agree that the possibility of Noah building such a structure must have been a supernatural undertaking. You may also agree that Genesis 1:2 may not have been the first or only time the earth was in that state.

Now let's consider the flood itself. If the waters above merged with the waters below, where exactly was the ark? Unless it was a submarine, which I doubt it was.

The original work for ark is *"tebah"* which is the same word used for the vessel that Moses was put in as a baby. So, an ark is possibly more than just a physical structure, in the same way you are more than a physical being.

The agreement between two and three referenced in Matthew 18 is an arcing principle for the manifestation of God, where you are able to operate in multiple realms. I will continue to say "multiple realms" to lift our consciousness to that level. There are multiple realms of reality; even your dream life alludes to this. We cannot keep seeing reality from just the earthly or demonic realm. There are many other realms.

It is possible that the ark, in both cases of Noah and Moses, was able to travel in and out of this realm, in the same way the children of Israel were not always visible to their enemies as they travelled with the ark of the covenant. The ark represented access to other realms.

Jesus said something interesting in John 10:9 **"I am the door: by me if any man enter in, he shall be saved and shall go in and out and find pasture."**

The root word for *saved* there means to deliver, protect, heal, preserve, be made whole. If I should really push this, Jesus was the door to the ark that only God could shut or open. Again we try to visualize this in terms of physicality without questioning how it was that only God could close and open the door in that era.

Noah was born for this purpose. Some other writings give a very interesting back story. Noah was 500 years old before he had his boys. He knew the earth was going to be destroyed and saw no point in having children. It was God who told him to go get a wife.

Noah was born talking and levitating. His father, Lamech, was afraid and went to discuss it with his father, Methuselah. It is written that Methuselah went to the ends of the earth to find his father, Enoch. This was about thirty years before Enoch was translated from this realm, yet Enoch could not be found in this realm. Methuselah knew how to find him.

Enoch told Methuselah everything that was going to happen. Lamech and Methuselah also knew the earth would be destroyed.

Noah knew his purpose, and I see a lot of similarities between him and Adam, for example, the animals were brought to him.

According to Genesis 7:23, every living substance was destroyed, meaning no longer in existence. The waters prevailed on the earth for 150 days.

Let me stretch your mind even more.

In Genesis 8:1, the word "wind" is used there. This is the same exact word used for "Spirit" in Genesis 1:2, which means there was a hovering of the Spirit as it was in the beginning. The Spirit of God was moving on the face of the waters, which was a precursor to creation, particularly the trees and plants, etc.

If God did not find one righteous human being on earth, there would have been a total destruction and a full recreation of humanity. So, what is evident is that Noah was created like Adam.

Noah sent out a dove who found no rest until after the seven days. The dove came back with an olive leaf in her mouth. If all living substance was destroyed by the flood, it means there was a re-creation just prior to Noah and his family leaving the ark. There was no one on earth to plant a tree, nor can you get a tree from a seed in seven days, unless by divine intervention. So, what we witness here is a repetition of Genesis 1:11.

Then Noah built an altar to the Lord, and took of every clean animal and of every clean bird, and offered burnt offerings on the altar. And the Lord smelled a soothing aroma. Then the Lord said in His heart, "I will never again curse the ground for man's sake, although the imagination of man's heart is evil from his youth; nor will I again destroy every living thing as I have done." (Genesis 8:20-21 - NKJV).

It is funny how we seldom give much intellectual thought to text like this. In the context of God being Spirit, for Him to smell anything makes no sense. Spirit doesn't have a nose or the capacity to smell anything. We are also talking about the burning flesh of animals, which is not a pleasing aroma on any level.

If you look at the original language, the word used for smell is *"ruach,"* which is the same word for spirit. A sacrifice made from a right place becomes a spirit that delights the heart of the Father. This is why Cain's offering was not accepted. It is not about the offering itself but the heart behind the sacrifice. If you give anything, even to God, from a wrong place, you create a demon that you end up going to war with. Your heart is the determining factor to what pleases God, not what you do or with what you do it.

Note also that the ground was no longer cursed. So the curse of the ground when Adam fell and the curse of the ground when Cain fell was removed. This is a brand new start for humanity because of one man.

Another similarity between Noah and Adam is found in Genesis 9:1-3. The keywords there are 'Be fruitful, multiply and replenish." Noah was not told to subdue the earth as Adam was.

Another similarity between Noah and Adam was the uncovering of Noah's nakedness (see Genesis 9:20-25). Why was Noah so angry with Ham? What was the big deal?

We see this uncovering of nakedness when Adam fell. God gave them coats of skin, which means, technically, they would have still been physically naked. I know we have this image of them wearing leaves sown together around their genitals, and nothing I say might remove that image from your mind, but there is a covering that God provides for a certain level of nakedness that should only be exposed to God. Adam and Eve wore this covering, and Noah also wore it. We actually see this garment being passed down throughout scripture. Have you ever wondered why Joseph's brothers were so angry with him for getting that coat of many colours? It was actually a means of access, which is why Joseph could see the future.

The idea of wearing clothes in the physical stems from the reality of being naked and without covering in the spiritual. Your soul/spirit does not wear clothes, yet if I see you in that realm, you are not naked. What are you wearing? What is covering your nakedness? Do you actually think there is a seamstress in the heavens giving clothes to human beings when they get there?

I want to push this even further, just for the fun of it. If I do anything else by doing this, I hope I am causing you to think. We wear clothes to mostly cover up our private parts, but we are allowed to expose these areas to the one we are in a covenant relationship with. Why? Because we have become one with this person. So our union with God means there is a version of you that is exclusively His, and you are not permitted to uncover that version of you for anyone, so He gives you a covering to hide a nakedness that only He alone is permitted to see. This was Ham's sin.

If God gave Adam and Eve coats of skin, and then gave them a covering, what would that look like? What would it mean for the one wearing it?

As we traverse scripture, mantles start showing up. Elijah had a mantle. It seemingly contained power. This trend continues throughout scripture.

When Noah uncovered himself, his son saw his true form, which was supposed to be hidden.

Then came Nimrod, who was born from the lineage of Ham. The Bible says he was a mighty hunter before the Lord, but what was he hunting? Some writings say Nimrod wanted to avenge his forefathers by building a tower so high, if God brought another flood, it would not destroy them. Talk about the power of one. Nimrod needed great manpower to accomplish that, so it is said he was a hunter of souls or a hunter of men.

Nimrod established the kingdom of Bael, which is connected to Nineveh and Sodom and Gomorrah. The Canaanites also came from Ham, and we know from them came a lot of the enemies of God.

Genesis 10 ends with the earth being divided into different families, tongues, lands and nations. Genesis 11 starts with the whole earth having one language. How was this accomplished?

Nimrod was the son of Cush, who was the son of Ham. Whatever garment Noah was wearing when he uncovered himself was taken by Ham, which is why Noah was upset. It was not just about seeing him naked. Nimrod was given this garment by his father. The Bible says in some translations that he became the world's first great conqueror.

Nimrod succeeded in bringing the earth that was divided into nations and languages under one rule and one language. They then decided to build the tower of Babel, which was a huge multi-dimensional structure. Some writings say it was so high, they shot an arrow upwards and it came back down with blood on it.

Nimrod was no ordinary guy. We need to consider the possibility that there are garments made by God that give human beings dominance. Paul keeps telling us in New Testament writings to "Put on.." and "Put off.." I believe we are yet to learn the mystery of garments.

We know Elijah's mantle went to Elisha. What happened to it afterward? Joseph had a coat of many colours. His brother's had to remove the coat to do what they wanted to do to him. John the Baptist wore a particular clothing. People may say I am reading too much into Scripture, but these same people are not reading into it at all. If you check it, at the very core, they actually have no idea what the Bible is talking about.

The tower of babel was built to reach into "hashamayim" (the heavens). This heaven may not be in this dimension. Science has discovered billions of galaxies in our physical world that span many light years across, but have not found a place called "heaven" outside of the cosmos. There are heavens that are not in this dimension. So this tower was more than a physical structure. We are talking about portals and dimensional travel, which means that the knowledge of how to access these realms was still on the earth. The tower did not need to reach beyond the galaxies to hashamayim, which means the heavens are much closer than we think, but we have to think dimensional. Where does the immortal soul of a believer who dies go?

Jesus did say the kingdom of heaven is near.

Let's note something here. The Bible says the name of the Lord is a strong tower. The righteous run into it and are safe (see Proverbs 18:10).

The tower of babel then was a replica or a counterfeit version of something true. If they had succeeded, the human race would have been lost.

But the Lord came down to see the city and the tower which the sons of men had built. And the Lord said, "Indeed the people are one and they all have one language, and this is what they begin to do; now nothing that they propose to do will be withheld from them. Come, let Us go down and there confuse their language, that they may not understand one another's speech." So the Lord scattered them abroad from there over the face of all the earth, and they ceased building the city. (Genesis 11:5-8 - NKJV).

"Came down" suggests a descent "to see." So, for the Lord to "see" what the men on earth were doing, He had to descend. We see this descending again with Abraham and the city of Sodom and Gomorrah.

Listen what God says:

Behold, the people is one, and they have all one language; and this they begin to do: and now nothing will be restrained from them, which they have imagined to do. (Genesis 11:6 - KJV).

This is God speaking about a people who have undertaken an impossible task that He did not commission or approve of them doing. So humanity is capable of far more than we realize.

The name Babel means confusion. From Babel, we get Babylon, Babylonian, etc., so Babel/Babylon is not a place. The people's language was confounded, and they were scattered across the face of the earth, the very thing they were trying to avoid. So they had prophetic insight. It means as well that Babylon is a system run by people and not the people themselves. Babylon can be considered a counterfeit version of the kingdom of God, which is ruled by men who want to establish a rule and government on earth independent of God or God's people.

Throughout this chapter, we see that one man can save a world, and one man can cause its destruction. This is the power embedded in us, and how we use it is incumbent on our will.

You can change this world for better or for worse, and indirectly or directly, you will. If your will is surrendered to God's will, you become a force to reckon with. Know thyself, thou son of God.

Chapter 5

PERCEPTION VERSUS REALITY

A study of the book of Job reveals many things, but I think a central theme of this entire chapter is perception versus reality. In other words, what we think is going on versus what is really happening. This is something I grew up with in church; we develop a language for things we really know nothing about. But Job sets the record straight, if we allow him to.

The world as we know it seems excessively chaotic. Then there are many voices going out into the world, which means there are many perceptions abounding and contributing to the reality many of us live with without realizing we have the power to change it by changing our perception. If we think God is going to destroy the world based on how we read the scriptures, then whether that is true or not, it becomes our reality. Does that mean God is going to really destroy the world because we think He is?

Our perception of self, others, and God play a vital role in framing the reality we experience from day to day, but just because we believe something to be true does not make it true.

God, or even you, cannot be truly known by study alone but by revelation. God must reveal you or reveal Himself to you for both to be truly known. Otherwise, we are just beating the air and forming patterns of thoughts and beliefs that have no real foundation. This is why Biblical writers walked in the level of spirituality they walked in that we are yet to. They were able to engage and experience what was authentic, so they didn't have to make things up.

The book of Job is a good study on this.

I was told the story of a well-known theologian that we still use his material today. He wrote many apologetics. One day, Jesus appeared to him. When he came out of that experience, the first thing he said was, "Burn all my books." It is really hard to capture God in a book in the same way this book you hold in your hand doesn't fully encompass the whole being of who I am as the author. You have to experience knowing me to know me, not just read my book. It is for this reason that I have separated the written Word of God from the living Word of God, and I believe the Bible supports me doing this.

Most believers know God by what they have heard, read, or seen, not by revelation. There is a perception of God established by the knowledge of God on the earth today that differs from person to person, and so many think they are right and everyone else is wrong. This is the same thing we see playing out in the book of Job.

His friends, Zophar, Eliphaz, and Bildad each had their own perception of who God is and what was happening to Job. Their religious background may have contributed to them seeing God from a certain perspective, so they projected that into Job's immediate dilemma: Job must have done something wrong for

God to be punishing him. Job's perspective, on the other hand, was quite different. He had no knowledge of what he may have done wrong, so God was seemingly acting unjustly toward him. Note, none of these guys knew about the conversation God had with satan. So none of their arguments was based on the factual reality of what had transpired in the unseen world.

In Job 19:3, Job made a statement that his friends had attacked him ten times. Ten is a very interesting number we see repeated through scripture. Abraham was tested ten times. There were ten plagues in Egypt. God spoke ten times to create the world. Tithing is 10% of your increase. The list can go on and on.

When I looked at the scripture, I could only identify five times when his friends spoke to him. How did Job identify this as ten shameless attacks?

The accusations against Job were as follows:

- God has blocked his way and shrouded his path in darkness.

- Stripped him of honor, removed the crown from his head.

- Tears him down on every side and uproots his hope.

- God is angry with him and considers him his enemy.

- Cut him off from his relatives and close friends.

Was any of this true?

Job had spent his entire life to this point serving a God he had never met. His perception of God was only flawed by the lack of knowledge he had about his true self. He knew that one encounter with God could set the record straight, and he was willing to wait for that.

If we cannot see our value and worth in God, we will never be able to truly see God for who He is. I can tell a believer who is on the journey to knowing God because they speak well of themselves and others. You cannot have a right perception of God and a flawed perception of self.

Job's friends thought they knew God. They believed wholeheartedly that they were correct in their analysis of what was happening to their friend to the point where they believed they spoke for God.

Job never spoke for God because he knew God could speak for Himself. The flaw in Christendom today is that everyone wants to speak for God and defend a God they have never truly had a direct encounter with.

As I studied Job's friends, it was revealed that they were learned men; they were very articulate and had a language for their knowledge. So what did they lack? They had never had an encounter with God. If you read every book I have ever written, can you say you know me, if you have never had a telephone conversation with me or met me in person? So how can we know God just by reading? Yes, He is the Author, and the Word of God epitomises a revelation of Him to those who wrote down their experiences, but this means you have a book to write in the great book of life as well. How will your chapters read? What experiences with God can you document?

The reality is, we cannot know God, or ourselves, in the flesh. It makes sense now what Paul says:

Wherefore henceforth know we no man after the flesh: yea, though we have known Christ after the flesh, yet now henceforth know we him no more. Therefore if any man be in Christ, he is a new creature: old things are passed away; behold, all things are become new. (2 Corinthians 5:16–17 — KJV).

Job or us never walked with Jesus in the flesh for us to know Him from that perspective. It means then that if the world of Spirit is real, then it must be experienced by spirit. So, the new that we have become is not after the flesh but spirit. Our perception of spirit from the perspective of flesh will always be flawed.

So one lesson in all this is that we stay humble with the knowledge we have until our day of visitation comes. Say like Paul, **"That I may know Him…"** Paul had awesome encounters with God, but he knew that the path to knowing God is from faith to faith and from glory to glory experientially, not by acquired knowledge alone.

We must believe that God is until He reveals who He is. Encounters with God are vital to the journey of sonship and understanding our own embedded divinity. It will come to those who wait for it.

We are all children of God, born from above. There are many children in the kingdom of God but few sons. As my mentor reiterates, **"A child is born; a son is given."** Sons are forged through perpetually experiencing God as Spirit. If you are like me, this process is really difficult because every time God initiates a spiritual encounter, we get consumed with fear. That is a topic for another time.

Our walk with God must be rooted in authenticity. Don't make things up. We can declare the Word of God and have expectations but don't speak a reality you have not confirmed by experience. We must not be afraid to be honest with where we are so God can move us to where we were destined to be.

I remember having a difficult season and trying to meditate and do a daily devotion. It was hard on some days because I could not focus. In the midst of engaging one night, I became totally honest with God about where I was. I apologize for bringing my frustration into that moment, but God responded. The next morning, He initiated an experience I had not had for a long time, but I was too afraid to see it through.

Note Job's enunciation:

For the thing I greatly feared has come upon me, and what I dreaded has happened to me. I am not at ease, nor am I quiet; I have no rest, for trouble comes. (Job 3:25-26 - NKJV).

Could it be that God allows us to go through certain realities to strip us of fear so we can experience a greater measure of Him as a living being?

Perception has been a big topic of conversation and motivational talks in the last couple of decades. I realize that as I study the book of Job, what we perceive to be reality may not be THE reality.

You cannot know God by study alone but by encounters. This was established from the very beginning. Adam and Eve knew God by experience. If we claim to know God by study alone, then that can become a hindrance to us having real encounters with the real God. Many people miss their moment of visitation because God never came to them in the way God is perceived by them to be.

One Christian mystic father says he believes every single believer will encounter Jesus in person at least once while on earth.

With the onset of the COVID-19 virus, we entered a new age. Much has changed; how we do business, school, etc., but I note that many churches seemed to have pressed the "pause" button. Many churches have lost regular attending members who have either stopped coming or opted to join services online. What is remarkable is that the church seems to be the only organization that was waiting for COVID-19 to disappear so they can get back to the "norm."

Why are we always lagging behind? Why do we resist changing the dynamics of how we do things to fit the age we are in? Why do we keep looking back? Why is our response to a new age reality to always look back to what was or pretend the present reality is not happening for real?

As believers, we must learn to always be in tune with the heart and mind of God because that is what we are charged to manifest as reality, not our own perception of what is or what should be. The living Word of God is always current because in Him we live, move, and have our being. It is the Word that holds matter in place and keeps reality in existence. Perception is our interpretation of what that reality is, and seeing wrong can cause us to create counter realities that are nothing but a temporary illusion. We must cease functioning from an age that has passed.

Job was not being encouraged by his friends. They were more accusatory in their perception of what was happening. Job disagreed and defended his purity. He felt like he was being punished for no cause. In the midst of our pain and trauma, it can be hard to see correctly and interpret the "good" in the chaos.

Job says the wicked prosper and are well off (see Job 21). This is similar to David's cry in the midst of his own troubles. The wicked don't seem to have as much trouble as the believer does, and this can cause us to see a reality that is not. There is always more happening than what we see manifesting in our immediate environment.

There is a conflict within the believer that is not necessarily found in the wicked. They have already made their choice, and their fate is sealed. Conflict arises when one determines to be righteous because the true self will always be at odds with the false self for dominance. It is a mortal weakness to struggle with letting go of what was. This rising conflict creates the experiences we go through.

There was a greater version of Job that would emerge from his experience, but he could not see it. Maybe he was not meant to as we are. There is no necessity for a wicked person to go through this process. I find that as you traverse the different levels or dimensions of maturity, the internal battle intensifies.

Eliphaz's perception of Job was very interesting (see Job 22:4-11), but was Job really guilty of any of this? Sometimes the opinion that people have of you is not even based on facts.

In Job 22:21-23, we see where the friends are convinced that they are speaking for God. Were they? But Job had questions he knew only God could answer (see Job 23:7-12). Job also knew who he was to the point of affirming his right standing with God. We can never respond correctly to the circumstances we face unless we know who we are. As long as our perception is filtered through a false lens, our perception is going to be wrong. Job knew he was righteous because he chose to be.

Bildad had a very personal opinion on humanity (see Job 25:4-6). The church has built its doctrine on this point of view. We have the language to enunciate such. Interestingly, Job's response to this is to declare God's greatness (see Job 26). How can a great God come to possess the body of a vile creature, and the creature remains vile? Job cemented his integrity on the merit of who he knew God to be.

Though our circumstances change, for the better or for the worse, God remains the same. There is a truth about you and me that is not skewed by what we are going through but remains intact because it is embedded in who God is. So, at the core of our experiences is an unchangeable truth, which is God Himself.

Job knew God (see Job 28), not the way we know Him today by reading and what others have told us. Job speaks about the movement of God in creation, something we would know nothing about if Job had made no mention of it. How did Job come by this knowledge if not by experience? What was Job's problem then? If God is constant and never changes, and we live in a reality where the all-powerful God is not being manifested, then what is the problem? The same problem Job had, we have. This is revealed in Job 29-31. Job makes a final appeal in summary before going silent. He wanted his life to go back to what it was. Additionally, in Job 31, Job described himself as he knew himself by what he did, but Job did not really know himself as God knew him. God was about to introduce Job to his true self.

Keep in mind, the sons of God appeared before the Father, and satan was among them. Ignorance to who you really are can cause you to be out of place, and in that spot will always stand one who accuses you, even if that one is you.

Job knew who he was by what he did in this realm but not by who he was in the other realm. If Job knew who he was, it would have been him standing before God and not satan. What we do on earth is just a by-product of who we are in the other realm. We are not righteous here because we do the right things. We are righteous here because we are righteous there. There is nothing we do here that qualifies us for something there because we are already there (see Ephesians 2:6). We have just not yet been formally introduced.

Job didn't need a revelation of God. What he needed was a revelation of himself in God. We think the written Word is God revealing Himself to humanity. It is, but it is so much more. The

Bible's central theme is God becoming man, so it is a revelation of the God-man or the man or woman in God, as we so love to call each other today. It is not a play on words because that is who you are. To be engrafted into something is to become that which you are engrafted into. The reason we are not manifesting God in creation is that we really don't believe we are in Him.

What was the question God asked Adam when he fell? *"Where are you?"* It was not about his physical location. Something had changed, and he was out of place. What was the first question God asked Job when He finally spoke? *"Where were you…?"* It is easy to locate us physically, but where are we in the other realms? Are we where we are supposed to be? Our position there determines our level of manifestation here.

In Job 32-37, we see the youngest of the friends making his contribution. Again, there is a classic case of perceived reality versus actual reality.

We often say "God is God." There is a version of God that is actual, factual, and never changing. Do I know God at that level? I do not. Now, there are many variations as it relates to who God is… perceived reality. You can talk to twenty different people and get twenty different versions of God. The question is, which one is the real God? Each of these twenty people believes their perceived reality is right and everyone else is wrong or deceived. The reality is, we could all be wrong, or maybe we are all right.

I have a question for you: What is your perception of God based on? Because if you have not personally met God, if it is true that He is a person, then how can you say you know Him? Maybe it is this deception that hinders us from actually knowing Him.

97

The truth about God is known only by God-self. The Holy Spirit searches the deep things of God, according to Paul, and we have the Spirit, which means we have access to the depth of God. But does having information or even revelation about someone equate to knowing them?

There is a version of you that is like God, and similarly, it is true, factual, and unchanging. This real you is known by God. The challenge is, any perception we have of God or self that does not align with what is true and unchanging becomes a person who is real but not true.

We create, by the powers of perception, different versions of God and ourselves that become real for us but not true. This is what we see playing out in the book of Job.

No one knows God like God, but we assume to know God by knowledge and perception and not actually meeting God. So we create idols that we worship as God.

Likewise, no one knows you like God, which means to meet the real you, you have to meet the real God, so we create or settle for false versions of ourselves, living in a world or reality of our own making. In essence, we are idols serving idols.

I have found that the best path to knowing God is to give up what I think I know about God. It makes sense now what Paul says here:

Brethren, I do not count myself to have apprehended; but one thing I do, forgetting those things which are behind and

reaching forward to those things which are ahead. (Philippians 3:13 - NKJV).

He also said:

For I determined not to know anything among you except Jesus Christ and Him crucified. (1 Corinthians 2:2 - NKJV).

What Jesus did—the Word becoming flesh to redeem humanity—is a never-changing fact and should sit at the foundation of the believer's life. Our interpretation and perception of His ministry and what it means for us is malleable. Every time we think we have God all figured out, He will reveal an aspect of Himself that we have never seen before. When we kill the idols, the real God will be known.

The Job that Job knew was defined by his life's accomplishments and all that he did as a righteous man, but there was another Job that only God knew about. But before we get there, let's examine the arguments of the youngest friend.

He agrees with the others that Job must have acted wickedly, and his predicament was well justified. He believed Job was presumptuous to want an audience with God. He makes the assumption that God punishes people with sickness (see Job 33:19). Was God doing anything to Job? Does God correct us by sending sickness and filling our bodies with pain? From the bird's eye view that we are privileged to have of this story, we know none of that is true.

Elihu claims that his perception of God is true and Job's not (see Job 36:1-4). He literally says he is speaking on God's behalf, and we know that isn't true. Read the entire chapter of Job 36 to get an insight into Elihu's belief about who God is.

The language of believers many times is to use the name of God to validate our perceptions when in reality, we don't even know how God moves in creation.

In Job 37:1-5, there is a storm. This is how we interpret scenarios like this; we hear the lightning and say "That is God." We hear the thunder and say "That is God." We see the wind blowing, the clouds gathering, and say "There is God." We see water turning to ice and say "That must be God." The rain starts pouring, and we say "Either God is punishing us or showing us favour." We see the golden glow in the North and say "That must be the glory of God."

So Elihu makes his conclusion:

As for the Almighty, we cannot find Him; He is excellent in power, in judgment and abundant justice; He does not oppress. (Job 37:23 - NKJV).

If we jump back (or ahead) to the book of 1st Kings, we know God was not in the wind. He was not in the earthquake. God was not in the fire. But there was a soft whisper of a voice that said, **"Elijah, what are you doing here?'**

Reading through Job 36-37, one would think Elihu knew God. But he saw God as the lightning and thunder in the storm, as a force behind the formation of clouds and rain, as the force behind water turning into ice, and like his friends, he didn't know God as a person. There was no relationship.

When God finally spoke from the storm in Job 38 onwards, only Job heard his voice. The starting point in knowing God and knowing who you really are is to know the voice of God. This is not just about reading the Bible. That is a good practice, but you must get beyond that because the Living Word has never ceased speaking from the day of creation. The voice will lead you to the face, and in that place, you will begin to experience what is actual reality.

Chapter 6

BUILD ME A HOUSE

"Build Me A House" may seem like a paradox in light of the fact that we are already the "House of the Lord," but there is something here worth exploring and that is the idea that, in reality, the house exists, but on a practical plain, it still needs to be built. Consider the process of a physical house. First, the architect develops a tangible visual outline of the house. Some can even show what the finished product will look like. Developing the plans includes adding measurements, electrical and plumbing infrastructure, sewage, etc. In other words, there must be a finished imagery of a house and approval before construction can begin. The question we must ask is, "At what point did the house become real?" Is it at conception in the mind or when the house is actually formed in the physical environment? When is a baby real? Is it at conception or birth?

Paradoxes are fun to play with, and there are many of these in Scripture. For example, to live, one must be willing to die; the first will be last; to be a master, one must serve, etc. If this principle also applies to us being the house of God, so while the house exists by virtue of conception, then there may still be a need for the house to be built. Why else would there be a command to **"work out our own salvation with fear and trembling"** if there is no work to be done once salvation is accepted?

Jacob was on his way to his uncle when he had a divine and profound experience:

Now Jacob went out from Beersheba and went toward Haran. So he came to a certain place and stayed there all night, because the sun had set. And he took one of the stones of that place and put it at his head, and he lay down in that place to sleep. Then he dreamed, and behold, a ladder was set up on the earth, and its top reached to heaven; and there the angels of God were ascending and descending on it. And behold, the Lord stood above it and said: "I am the Lord God of Abraham your father and the God of Isaac; the land on which you lie I will give to you and your descendants. Also your descendants shall be as the dust of the earth; you shall spread abroad to the west and the east, to the north and the south; and in you and in your seed all the families of the earth shall be blessed. Behold, I am with you and will keep you wherever you go, and will bring you back to this land; for I will not leave you until I have done what I have spoken to you." Then Jacob awoke from his sleep and said, "Surely the Lord is in this place, and I did not know it." And he was afraid and said, "How awesome is this place! This is none other than the house of God, and this is the gate of heaven!" (Genesis 28:10-17 - NKJV).

It is believed that what Jacob was referring to as the house of God was his location at the time. He responded to that revelation by creating an altar with the stone on which he laid, pouring oil on it, and making a vow to the Lord. This is a profound experience laced with mystical connotations and mystery.

The interpretation that the house of God referenced by Jacob became clearer centuries later when Jesus had an equally profound conversation with one of His potential disciples at the time:

Jesus saw Nathanael coming toward Him, and said of him, "Behold, an Israelite indeed, in whom is no deceit!" Nathanael said to Him, "How do You know me?" Jesus answered and said to him, "Before Philip called you, when you were under the fig tree, I saw you." Nathanael answered and said to Him, "Rabbi, You are the Son of God! You are the King of Israel!" Jesus answered and said to him, "Because I said to you, 'I saw you under the fig tree,' do you believe? You will see greater things than these." And He said to him, "Most assuredly, I say to you, hereafter you shall see heaven open, and the angels of God ascending and descending upon the Son of Man." (John 1:47-51 - NKJV).

The deeper revelation embedded in this text is that what Jacob saw was himself as the house of God on the earth. The Bible makes it succinctly clear that we are now the temple of the Holy Spirit (Who is God).

Do you not know that you are God's temple and that God's Spirit dwells in you? (1 Corinthians 3:16 - ESV).

Without question, we are the temple of God, but is the house complete, or is there still a need for construction? Could there be a similarity here with the process necessary for the establishment of a physical structure on the earth?

God is seeking for a place not built with human hands to occupy. It is not just making a space for Him in our lives but also building a structure where He can fully dwell within the framework of who we really are as a redeemed human being. We may say our bodies are not big enough to contain God, but can we truly measure our capacity to hold God by just the physical structure we call the body when the mind is so expansive and contains the whole created universe? I would say "beyond," but most of us cannot push our minds to think beyond the created world to begin to fathom what exists there. There is nothing there...yet.

The process of Christianity, particularly coming into maturity, can be likened to building a physical house. First, there must be a blueprint, which gives an idea of what the finished product will look like and the process needed for the successful completion of the building. There are plans with specific measurements and guidelines to follow. The building must be completed conceptually before construction even begins. If we are the house of God, then what does that house look like? How is it intended to function? Where is it located? What purpose does it serve?

Next, a foundation needs to be established. This requires digging and concretizing, putting in the steelwork, marking off boundaries, making divisions, etc.

Next, the walls must be built, the floor must be cast, and the roof must be established. This part of the process tends to move rather quickly. Somewhere along this process, the plumbing and lighting will be installed. This is a key part of the process of building that will mostly be hidden in the final analysis. We will not see the wires and piping, but we will enjoy the functions they serve.

Then, finally, the refining process begins, and this is where great care and time is spent, and this takes up most of the time in the construction process.

But it is not the spiritual that is first but the natural, and then the spiritual. (1 Corinthians 15:46 - ESV).

Consider the above text in light of what is being discussed. With a physical building, the unseen is fully established before construction begins on what will be seen. When it comes to the believer, however, we already know our physical body is the temple of God, but is the spiritual counterpart automatically constructed? So there is a flip with how this works in both scenarios, even though the principles still apply.

Salvation via acceptance of the gospel message is the foundation of the believer's life. No matter what we do afterward, Jesus must remain at the very foundation of the structure we are attempting to establish for our Father. We must now build a spiritual house for God, and this requires great care.

God, who made the world and everything in it, since He is Lord of heaven and earth, does not dwell in temples made with hands. (Acts 17:24 – NKJV).

We are the house that was not built with human hands and the only physical being in creation that can house God, but it is more than just the physical being we are presently. This conclusion is drawn on the premise that most believers are not experiencing the full manifestation of the God who dwells in them as they walk out the redeemed path. A fully constructed house of God where God dwells fully would infuse even our shadows so that those with ailments can benefit without even our knowledge.

So that they even carried out the sick into the streets and laid them on cots and mats, that as Peter came by at least his shadow might fall on some of them. (Acts 5:15 - ESV).

Jesus took great care and a couple of years to build up His disciples to the point where they could house as much of God as He Himself carried.

However, the Most High does not dwell in temples made with hands, as the prophet says: 'Heaven is My throne, and earth is My footstool. What house will you build for Me? says the Lord, or what is the place of My rest?' (Acts 7:48-49 - NKJV).

The Bible is the blueprint, and we are the co-contractors in building God's house, and the house is you.

So, the cliché "under construction" is correct. Let's build God a house.

Chapter 7

MANIFESTING GOD

The goal of becoming a Christian is to manifest God in creation. As a matter of fact, the reason God created man in His image and likeness is so that He could experience His physical created world through us.

John 4:24 says God is Spirit (NKJV). I think we forget that sometimes. God is Spirit, and Spirit cannot experience the physical world unless He becomes a physical being, so when you say yes to Jesus, the Godhead inhabits your body. Why? So He has a channel through which He can manifest Himself in creation.

So, let's explore this. As usual, I will begin from the beginning:

Then God said, "Let the earth bring forth grass, the herb that yields seed, and the fruit tree that yields fruit according to its kind, whose seed is in itself, on the earth"; and it was so. And the earth brought forth grass, the herb that yields seed according to its kind, and the tree that yields fruit, whose seed is in itself according to its kind. And God saw that it was good. So the evening and the morning were the third day." (Genesis 1:11-13 - NKJV).

This is the history of the heavens and the earth when they were created, in the day that the Lord God made the earth and the heavens, before any plant of the field was in the earth and before any herb of the field had grown. For the Lord God had not caused it to rain on the earth, and <u>there was no man to till the ground</u>; (Genesis 2:4-5 – NKJV – emphasis mine).

The first thing we need to remember is that God did not need the worlds He created to be God. But for God to experience and govern the world He created, He needed to be a man. Or, let's use the safe language, He needed a man.

The second thing we need to know is that everything that existed, is existing, and will ever exist was already created by God. He already spoke it into existence. The Word is already there.

The Bible says: **Blessed *be* the God and Father of our Lord Jesus Christ, who has blessed us with <u>every spiritual blessing</u> in the heavenly *places* in Christ, just as He chose us in Him before the foundation of the world, that we would be holy and blameless before Him. In love. (Ephesians 1:3-4 – NASB – emphasis mine).**

Everything we need for life and godliness already exists, but it has not all been manifested. We struggle with this a little bit, right? Because sometimes we don't feel so blessed. The truth is, ALL things were already created in Spirit, so what has not yet manifested is locked up in God, until He can <u>find a man </u>who will manifest its reality.

There was no man to till the ground…no man to cultivate the ground…no man to manifest what God has already spoken into existence. Why do you think God brought the animals to Adam to name them? Did you know that the animals did not take physical form until Adam named them? The Bible says whatsoever Adam called every living creature, that *was* the name thereof.

You will also declare a thing, and it will be established for you; so light will shine on your ways. (Job 22:28 - NKJV).

Let me read a part of a Jewish document that I found interesting: Here is a quote from the Midrash to Genesis 2:19:

When the Holy One, blessed be He, was about to create humankind, He consulted with His ministering angels, saying, "Let us make Adam." The angels responded, "What's so wonderful about this Adam?" So He brought each creature before the angels and asked them, "This creature, what is its name?" But they did not know. Then He brought the creatures before Adam and asked him, "This creature, what is its name?" To which Adam responded, "This is *shor* [Hebrew for ox], this is *chamor* [donkey]..."

Adam was able to perceive the spiritual components of the creative spirit that brought every animal into being, and named each animal in conjunction with its spiritual configuration.

You were a Word spoken before the foundation of the world. When your parents came together, you manifested. Without a man, nothing from that realm can manifest in this world.

So the order we see in creation is that God, who is Spirit, speaks, creating the spiritual component of what He wants to establish in creation, and man, on whom the Spirit is given without measure, manifests it in the physical world.

The problem we have is not that God is not speaking, but man is not manifesting. I always ask, "Why did God save you and give you His Holy Spirit? Why has God deposited in us the gifts of the Spirit and the fruit of the Spirit? Why did Jesus pray in John 17 that the same oneness that exists in the Godhead will also exist between Himself and us?"

Do you really think God did all that just to save you from hell? Hell was not even created for you. In the beginning God created the heavens and the earth. Heavens—plural—many heavens, not just one.

I believe that the man and woman created as living souls shared in the nature of the Godhead. Because of their oneness with the Father, they were able to manifest God in creation in a powerful way, as if God was doing it Himself. Whatever God spoke, the man would manifest it. So the verse that says God rested from all His work that He has done, in the original language, as my mentor teaches, should read, God rested from all the work that He has created to be done.

God, who is Spirit, was now manifested in a physical being called Adam (man), who was given dominion and rule over the created world. When man fell, the union was broken.

I want you to see something here. This is important.

Because man fell, there was no MAN to GOVERN the created world. No man. I know we teach that the dominance was passed on to satan, but satan is not a physical being, so unless he inhabits the body of a physical being, he really cannot govern the physical world, which is why, by the way, he may have been fighting for the body of Moses.

By divine design, God's idea, not mine, there needed to be a man who would govern the created world, so if the first Adam failed, there arose a need for a second Adam.

In the beginning was the Word, and the Word was with God, and the Word was God. He was in the beginning with God. All things were made through Him, and without Him nothing was made that was made. In Him was life, and the life was the light of men. And the light shines in the darkness, and the darkness did not comprehend it. And the Word became flesh and dwelt among us, and we beheld His glory, the glory as of the only begotten of the Father, full of grace and truth. (John 1:1-5, 14)

God became Man, and the governance and dominion that rested on the first Adam, now sat on the second Adam. The prophet Isaiah testified that:

Of the increase of His government and peace there will be no end... (Isaiah 9:7a - NKJV).

It means then that there is a Man in the Godhead who now governs all things in the created world, and there is nothing or no one that can ever dethrone Him.

But there is something else: in the loins of the first Adam was the entire human race. So when he fell, we all fell; every single human being born into this world is born from the seed of the first Adam.

What happens when you get saved and say yes to Jesus is that God inserts you into His Son, so when Jesus was crucified, you were crucified. When He died, you died. When He rose, you rose. And when He ascended, He took you into the Godhead, so now you are seated with Christ in heavenly places.

Jesus is referred to as the second Adam or some texts will say the Last Adam. He is the guarantee that this version of humanity WILL NOT FAIL. No matter how bad the world gets, or how chaotic, or how destructive, WE WILL NOT FAIL because Christ in us, the hope of glory.

You are in Christ, and Christ is in you. You are made partakers of God's divine nature. So now you share in His governance of the created world. You share in His dominion, His Power, and His influence in creation to change realities. This is why you can heal the sick; you can cast out demons, you can speak in heavenly tongues, you can raise the dead. You have the power to make the blind see, the dumb speak, the deaf hear, to deliver those who are held captive in regions of captivity.

There are two things that hinder a believer from manifesting God:

- Immaturity
- Ignorance—not a lack of knowledge, but ignoring what you should know.

You already have the faith. It doesn't take that much faith to manifest God.

I am immature. I am a child, but for some reason, I was taught as a son because God wanted me to have certain knowledge. But I struggle to manifest what I know to be true, because I am not yet a son, I am a child, but I have the knowledge of a son. I believe the Bible, and it says we can speak to the dead and see them come back to life. We can say to the cripple, rise up and walk. We can speak to the blind man so he receives his sight. We can open the ears of the deaf and loose the tongue of the dumb.

You have the power to manifest God in creation because when you got saved, God took you back before the beginning and inserted you into the perfect man before the fall, deposited in you Himself as Spirit, gave you gifts, gave you the fruit of the Spirit, gave you the power to trample on snakes and scorpions, gave you the power to cast out demons, heal the sick, raise the dead, break the chains of those who are in bondage, then sent you back here to manifest His glory on the earth.

Oh, you thought God was just saving you from hell? Most Christians don't know why heaven rejoices when they get saved. It's not about hell. You become this new creature who literally carries God in you. This is not a metaphor.

God saved you to restore you to what was originally in His mind when He said, **"Let us make man in Our image and likeness."**

We have turned Christianity into just another religion, and it has completely messed us up because we constantly diminish the will of God in creation. God wants to manifest Himself through you.

If this is not the case, then why would God pursue you to the ends of the world? Why would God even bother to become a human being? Why would the God of all creation insert Himself into you?

The world we live in is ever-expanding. New galaxies are being discovered every day. New planets. In the beginning God created the heavens and the earth, yet, on the earth, there are over eight billion human beings alive, and most of us don't even know the thoughts and plans God has for us. His plans for us are so big that He has to keep it a secret because we couldn't handle it because we have allowed our minds to be so congealed by religion.

But God is looking for a man who will manifest His will, His thoughts, His desires, His Word, and His culture in creation **"On earth, as it is in heaven."**

Will you answer the call?

Chapter 8

WHAT IS MAN?

God made man in His image and likeness. We always start here; this is the ending point, and the end is always a beginning. The mystics would say that God made a replica of Himself in creation—or extended a physical version of Himself in creation.

Man was given a function—what he was expected to do—roles and responsibilities; a son inherits his father's estate, so the created heavens and earth are a man's inheritance. I say "created" because there must be a heaven that was not created because that is where God lives. The heavens and earth in Genesis and subsequently throughout scripture were created.

Genesis summarizes a man's role in two verses:

Then God said, "Let Us make man in Our image, according to Our likeness; let them have dominion over the fish of the sea, over the birds of the air, and over the cattle, over all the earth and over every creeping thing that creeps on the earth." (Genesis 1:26)

Then God blessed them, and God said to them, "Be fruitful and multiply; fill the earth and subdue it; have dominion

over the fish of the sea, over the birds of the air, and over every living thing that moves on the earth." (Genesis 1:28).

This is not really as specific as we would want, but once God's rest ended, man was now in charge of the created world. His work began on day 8.

This means that when man fell, man was absolved of all his responsibilities. He was incapable of doing what he was created to do—literally. He lacked the capacity to carry out his function by virtue of the fall. The question to ask is, "If man was not doing what he was created to do, then who was now doing it?"

Before we can even answer this question, we need to at least have an idea of what a man in his original estate was able to do.

What does rule and dominion look like?

At face value, this is not clear, and the canon of the Bible does not help, unless you know what to look for. You must dig deeper to unearth the mystery embedded in Scripture.

Moses wrote the first five books of the Bible called the "Torah," but there is another book that Moses also wrote. The Bible in Chronological order (based on timelines) looks like this:

1. Genesis 1-11
2. Job 1-42
3. Genesis 12-50

So there must be something in the book of Job that has a more direct relation to man than where the book was positioned in the

Bible. Job lived before Abraham, and Moses was able to document this man of God's life.

The book of Job actually gives us a comprehensive listing of what man can do in his original estate.

Job is not really a lesson on enduring suffering, and neither is it making a statement that we should all suffer at that magnitude. Neither is his story about getting double for your trouble. Job is a revelation of original intent. When God began to speak in Job 38, every wrong perception of who God is and who we are began to melt away. Job and his four friends all served God, yet only Job heard the voice of God.

The language is very interesting in Job 38:1-3, **"Gird up now your loins like a man…"** The proper interpretation of this is "I, God, am about to tell you who a man really is." Before we go forward, let's go backward a little.

God created a world, and the last thing He made was a human being. Human beings are a physical manifestation and revelation of God in creation because we were made in His image and likeness, so there are some similarities there. We question this, but the same principle is embedded in our capacity to reproduce. Humans reproduce humans; God produces…. Yes, you get the picture. So, if God was a physical being, He would be a human being. This was God's idea, not ours. Humanity was supposed to represent God in creation as a son over his Father's estate.

God didn't create the world for Himself. Why would a supreme being who has been in existence for eons just finally decide He needed a world? He created a world; then He created the human being as an extension of Himself so He could govern and experience the world He created. We were made to function in a particular way and given responsibilities of governing, rule, and dominion. But something happened.

Man fell.

Think, downgrade.

Due to the fall, man was incapable of carrying out his function and responsibilities. This means someone else had to do what humanity was created to do so creation could be sustained.

There are two trains of thoughts here:

1. Either God created other beings to temporarily carry out these functions until man was fully restored to his original estate.

2. God did it Himself.

Option two is not very practical because if God could do what He created man to do as man does it, He would have no need for us. Why even bother to redeem us? There must be something about man that God would lower Himself to redeem us. God is Spirit, and for Spirit to operate in a physical environment as we do, they need a body. This is just a fact. If God wanted to do what He created man to do in creation, He would not have created us.

If man then is an expression of God-self, then man had become a fallen version of God-self, so God's love for humanity is a love of self, which is why God is love, and we can never be separated from love, unless we choose to be.

Hell is a wilful separation from God that seemingly cannot be remedied. We were not created to exist outside of God, so that alone is eternal punishment, even without the fire and brimstone.

So, the book of Job reveals man in all his glory. It shows what governing in creation looks like. There are things humanity knew how to do or was learning to do before the fall. Here's the issue: Because there was a descent of man, there has to be an ascent. There must be a going upwards until we become the full manifestation of who we were created to be. In your ascendency, you must never allow yourself to get stuck.

Job was okay with his life, until God intervened. God is the one who drew satan's attention to Job **"Have you considered my servant…?"** Why would God do that? Could it be He, seeing the bigger picture, saw an opportunity for the real Job to emerge? Yet, in the process of Job going through the refiner's fire, he wanted the life he had before. Wasn't this the same issue with the children of Israel? Even God said He had to send them another way because He knew that at the first sign of trouble, they would turn back.

It is easy to hold on to what we have because of our unsurety of what lies ahead. God promised us mansions, streets of gold, and total heavenly bliss, yet believers are afraid to die. Why is that? It is a mortal weakness to hang on to what has been and what it was because we don't know what is really ahead of us. God created us for more, but He has not told us what that is.

But as it is written: "Eye has not seen, nor ear heard, nor have entered into the heart of man the things which God has

prepared for those who love Him." (1 Corinthians 2:9 - NKJV).

We know there is nothing but great things ahead for us, but we don't know what it is, so we try to hold on to what we do know.

Let it go!

God created Job for more than what he settled for, and that is our problem today. We build ministries and tabernacles and settle for crumbs and milk and call it maturity and kingdom.

No believer can be settled in their mind that they are on the right path until they begin doing what Jesus did. A child knows nothing but milk from the day he/she is born. They have no idea what solid food is until they try it. Very soon, milk becomes a thing of the past. If we are to grow as believers, we need to try something different and something new.

I don't believe Christianity today is what it was meant to be. We have made it into an institution, and it has lost its organic essence. In other words, the church is an idol to many. When God gets involved in rectifying something, He will first destroy what it is so the real thing can emerge. All idols must be destroyed for that which is real to reveal itself.

Christianity and all other systems of the world will not survive the fire of God, but real humanity, the beings created as light by Light who bear the expressed image and likeness of God will stand when all idols fall.

If you settle for less than what God has for you, that thing becomes an idol. This is what happened to Job.

So now God speaks. In Job 38:4, the question is asked **"Where were you...?"** It seems this question has been asked by God since man fell because, apparently, we are seldom where we are supposed to be.

If satan appears among the sons of God before God, then who is he representing? Whose space is he occupying? Who has left that position vacant for him to be there?

We have this theology that says when man fell, the devil became the god of this world. Let's examine this. If he became the god of this world by virtue of the fall, it means man was originally the god of this world. Why did it have to be Jesus as a human being who took the keys and kingdom back from satan, if our theology is correct? Could it be because only a human being can do that? And why did Jesus give the keys back to you? Could it be because we had it before? Now that we are given the keys to the kingdom, who then is the god of this world now?

Every ill in our world today is executed by man. We like to blame devils, but the voice of satans and every other voice can only influence and tempt us to act. It is our actions that create the realities we are experiencing today; the good, bad and ugly. It means then that man must also be the remedy.

There is a progressiveness in scripture that we must be careful not to miss. The pre-resurrection reality that existed before Jesus was crucified and resurrected is quite different post-resurrection. Let us stop looking back and living a reality that no longer is.

Job 38-39 reveals man in his divine, original estate. I believe the listing here is all that Adam was able to do before he fell. When

123

God began to list these things to Job, like us, Job had no response. How could he respond when he knew nothing about what God was talking about? Let me just share just a part of what God said:

Then adorn yourself *with* majesty and splendor, and array yourself with glory and beauty. Disperse the rage of your wrath; look on everyone *who is* proud, and humble him. Look on everyone *who is* proud, *and* bring him low; tread down the wicked in their place. Hide them in the dust together, bind their faces in hidden *darkness*. Then I will also confess to you that your own right hand can save you. Look now at the behemoth, which I made *along* with you; He eats grass like an ox. (Job 40:10-15 - NKJV).

Let me say something here about the New King James Version. Here scholars tried to correct what was amiss in the King James Version, yet there are words still in this translation that are not in the original text. They highlight these in italics. I have italized them in the above text, so take another read. Try reading it without the italized words and see if you get the same essence.

Most translations of the Bible paint this picture that God is everything (which He is) and man is nothing (this is not really true). Man is nothing without God because man is a manifestation of God. When we choose not to have faith in God, we empty ourselves of God, leaving only a shell of what could have been. With God, the value of man is immeasurable because he is a house for the Lord. Everything changes about us when God comes to dwell in our temple.

Intrinsically man was made to do what God would do if He was a physical being in creation. So, essentially, God reveals to Job what was in His mind when He said, **"Let Us make man in Our image and likeness..."**

So, a man can:

- Command the morning; cause the dawn to know its place.

- Enter into the springs of the sea—walk in the recesses of the deep.

- Be familiar with the gates of death and deep darkness.

- Understand the expanse of the earth.

- Know the way to the dwelling of light.

- Know where darkness dwells, where is its place, take it to its territory, discern the paths to its home.

But of course you know all this! For you were born before it was all created, and you are so very experienced! (Job 38:21 - NLT).

We interpreted this text as sarcasm, but what if it is not? What if God was stating a fact?

A man can:

- Enter the storehouses of the snow.

- See the storehouses of the hail—reserved for the time of distress, and for the day of war and battle.

- Know the way that the light is divided, and the east wind that is scattered on the earth.

- Cleave a channel for the flood or a way for the thunderbolt.

- Bring rain on a land without people or a dessert without a man in it.

Man is 80% water, so water shows up wherever man shows up because he is a carrier of water.

Elijah was a man with a nature like ours, and he prayed fervently that it might not rain, and for three years and six months it did not rain on the earth. Then he prayed again, and heaven gave rain, and the earth bore its fruit. (James 5:17-18 - ESV).

Before any plant of the field was in the earth and before any herb of the field had grown. For the Lord God had not caused it to rain on the earth, and there was no man to till the ground; (Genesis 2:5 - NKJV).

There were no garden forks, clippers, pipes, hoses, or any of these tools, which means man was able to cultivate by how he was built to function without any external supplements.

Man can:

- Bring rain, even in a dessert, to satisfy the waste and desolate land, and make seeds of grass to sprout.

- Father the rain.

- Produce drops of dew.

- Produce ice and frost from heaven.

- Turn water into stone.

- Imprison the surface of the deep.

- Bind the chains of the Pleiades.

- Loose the cords of Orion.

- Lead forth a constellation in its season, and guide the bear with her satellites.

- Know the ordinances of the heavens.

- Fix their rule over the earth.

- Lift up your voice to the clouds so an abundance of water will cover you.

- Send forth lightnings that they may go and say to you, "Here we are."

- Put wisdom in the innermost being.

- Give understanding to the mind.

- Count the clouds by wisdom.

- Tip the water jars of the heavens when the dust hardens into a mass and the clods stick together.

- Hunt the prey for the lion.

- Satisfy the appetite of the young lions when they crouch in their dens and lie in wait in their lair.

- Prepare the raven its nourishment when its young cry to God and wander about without food.

- Know the time the mountain goats give birth.

- Observe the calving of the deer.

- Send out the wild donkey free.

- Loose the bonds of the swift donkey.

- Bind the wild ox in a furrow with ropes.

- Harrow the valleys after you.

- Give the horse his might—clothe his neck with a mane—make him leap like the locust.

- Command eagles.

There are more, but you get the idea.

We are not familiar with 99% of what is on this list. We may know about commanding the dawn; we know we can do this, but are we sure we know what we are doing when we do?

It becomes a challenge to know what spirituality is if we compare ourselves as we are now to the man before sin entered our context.

Because of Jesus, the possibility of building a house similar to the house that Adam was is possible—we all have the potential to be that.

Secondly, one will ask, "Isn't it God doing all these things?"

Who else could have taken on this role if man was no longer able to do them? Surely God made man in His image and likeness so man could carry out a specific role that God would be doing in creation. We cannot rule out the possibility that God does these things indirectly through man.

The son has the capacity to do what the Father does.

So Jesus said to them, "Truly, truly, I say to you, the Son can do nothing of his own accord, but only what he sees the Father doing. For whatever the Father does, that the Son does likewise." (John 5:19 - ESV).

The depth of the mystery embedded in this verse has gone unnoticed for a greater part of Christendom. The fact that the son has the capacity to do what the Father does speaks to the untapped potential within humanity. We are told to say yes to Jesus, but we are not given the full details of what we are saying yes to.

We don't know what heaven is like; we don't know what is waiting for us when or if we die. We don't know what our living and decisions are producing on the other side.

Saying yes to Jesus is our willingness to become that house for God, but then the house must be built.

Job had such a profound, enlightened experience that should have benefitted many generations following. Here is his response:

Then Job answered the Lord and said: "I know that You can do everything, and that no purpose of Yours can be withheld from You. You asked, 'Who is this who hides counsel without knowledge?' Therefore I have uttered what I did not understand, things too wonderful for me, which I did not know. Listen, please, and let me speak; You said, 'I will question you, and you shall answer Me.' "I have heard of You by the hearing of the ear, but now my eye sees You. Therefore I abhor myself, and repent in dust and ashes." (Job 42:1-6 - NKJV).

If you study scripture carefully, you will realize that it is not just a revelation of God in creation but a revelation of God becoming man. That is the central theme throughout: The Word becoming Flesh. If this is true, then you are also a word manifesting in time. What Job experienced will be the experience of every believer. If we don't get it in life, hopefully, we will get it in death.

Job says, "God, I see You."

> **Beloved, now we are children of God; and it has not yet been revealed what we shall be, but we know that when He is revealed, we shall be like Him, for we shall see Him as He is. (1 John 3:2 - NKJV).**

In seeing God, we see our true selves because we are a reflection of Him.

In Job 42, God rebuked the three friends mentioned in Job 2. Where was the fourth, Elihu? Elihu seems to have just appeared in Job 32. He was not mentioned in Job 2 or 42.

One Biblical commentator made a comparison between Elihu and the three friends. He cites two major differences in their speech:

1. The three friend's perspective, "Before you (Job) began suffering, you must have sinned."

2. Elihu's perspective, "Since you (Job) began suffering, you have sinned."

I found that quite interesting. Job never responded to Elihu, and God began speaking immediately after him.

The conclusion of the matter is, God has a goal in mind when it comes to His children, and He knows how to get us there. Stay the course and trust the process. God will order your steps according to His Word.

Chapter 9

THE SIN REMOVER

If you forgive the sins of any, they are forgiven them; if you retain the sins of any, they are retained. (John 20:23 - NKJV).

Do we have the power to forgive sins? According to Scripture, we do. The Bible specifically says "sin" in almost every translation, not offense—not what people do to you—but "sin." So, even if God forgives someone but you don't, the sin remains.

If we absolve ourselves of this responsibility, it is to the detriment of ourselves and others. Let's not be like the Scribes and Pharisees:

And the scribes and the Pharisees began to reason, saying, "Who is this who speaks blasphemies? Who can forgive sins but God alone?" But when Jesus perceived their thoughts, He answered and said to them, "Why are you reasoning in your hearts? Which is easier, to say, 'Your sins are forgiven you,' or to say, 'Rise up and walk'? But that you may know that the Son of Man has power on earth to forgive sins"—He said to the man who was paralyzed, "I say to you, arise, take up your bed, and go to your house." Immediately he rose up before them, took up what he had been lying on, and

departed to his own house, glorifying God. (Luke 5:21-25 - NKJV).

The "son of man" does have the power to forgive sins and heal anyone who may have been incapacitated because of their choices. I must admit though, this is not easy to do. From a mortal perspective, we want to see people punished for the sins they commit, though we ourselves want to be forgiven when we mess up. It is a terrible human discrepancy. People deserve our forgiveness, and the call on the believer's life is to act from their divinity and not from their mortality.

Jesus teaches us to forgive in Matthew 6:12:

Forgive us for doing wrong, as we forgive others. (Matthew 6:12 - CEV).

There is a correlation between us extending forgiveness and receiving it. By forgiving others, we remove their sin and ours.

Forgiveness is unconditional. Because of the interconnectedness of humanity, particularly those of us who are members of the body of Christ, anything we do or not do affects the whole.

As a side note, our perception plays a role in our capacity to forgive. The power of thought and belief does create our reality and shape the world we live in, whether it is a true reality or a false one. In our culture, we don't carve out idols from wood and stone, but we do shape them by thought and belief. But how far does our power extend? Can we deliver someone from death?

How do we view death today? Do we see it as final? Do we consider it to be an irreversible reality?

134

Jesus raised Lazarus from the grave four days after he died. From a scientific perspective, the body begins to decompose after three days. Additionally, the soul of Lazarus would have been long gone to wherever souls went at the time. The Jews believe you shouldn't try to raise anyone after the soul has long departed. The resurrecting of the dead after four days is an anomaly. Yet, Jesus says to us, "Do what I do."

Jesus sent his twelve harvest hands out with this charge: "Don't begin by traveling to some far-off place to convert unbelievers. And don't try to be dramatic by tackling some public enemy. Go to the lost, confused people right here in the neighborhood. Tell them that the kingdom is here. Bring health to the sick. Raise the dead. Touch the untouchables. Kick out the demons. You have been treated generously, so live generously." (Matthew 10:8 - MSG).

If we truly believe Jesus has given us the authority He has, then we have the power to release someone from death as well.

Let's dig a little deeper.

When someone dies, according to Ecclesiastes 12:7:

Life, lovely while it lasts, is soon over. Life as we know it, precious and beautiful, ends. The body is put back in the same ground it came from. The spirit returns to God, who first breathed it. (Ecclesiastes 12:7-8 - MSG).

This scripture doesn't enlighten us about what happens to the soul. So some doctrine teaches that the soul sleeps or no longer exists. My belief is a little bit different.

I believe the soul is the real you, and you are eternal. According to Scripture, you have to gain the whole world to lose your soul. So the value of one soul is equal to the whole world. The soul can die, according to Ezekiel 18:20, but it is not a death that renders the soul non-existent. The unbeliever operates from a dead soul in this world. Only believers are living souls. In both cases, the soul is immortal.

The Jews believe that after death, the soul hangs around for three days before departing. Where does it go?

Let's say the soul of the living goes to heaven. The living is the believer, according to Mark 12:27. So the soul of the dead goes to hell—the dead are the non-believers. If you raise a non-believer from the dead, have you not just delivered a soul from hell?

At the most basic, fundamental stage, when we get someone saved, we have pulled them from both death and hell. They are no longer counted among the dead but among the living. They are now a child of God—born from above.

So, we have the power to remove sin from the earth and deliver souls from death by virtue of our union with God. It is not God doing it independently of us but in partnership and union with us.

Why are we not manifesting more of God's power in the world if we have access to this much power?

As long as we separate ourselves from God in our language, perception, and belief, we will always function from a limited perspective. Jesus demonstrated for us that a son does what he sees the Father doing. God forgives, we forgive, and sin is removed.

We have the Holy Spirit. We have faith. We have all we need to operate as our Father in this world. So how can we, as faith-filled, Spirit-filled believers, do exactly what the Word says and nothing happens? I do have this question as well.

I look at the world and church and see a lot of suffering. If there is ever a need for the demonstration of the Spirit's power, it is now. There are great things happening in many parts of the world, and some are not public knowledge, but in my nation, we seem to predominantly fall in the category of **"having a form of godliness but denying the power thereof."** This is sad, and I pray that a remnant or a new generation will emerge that will create a different reality. People want to know that God is real, that He cares, and we, as children of God, bear this responsibility.

We need to see a manifestation of 1 Corinthians 4:20 in our nation:

I know there are some among you who are so full of themselves they never listen to anyone, let alone me. They don't think I'll ever show up in person. But I'll be there sooner than you think, God willing, and then we'll see if they're full of anything but hot air. God's Way is not a matter of mere talk; it's an empowered life. (1 Corinthians 4:20 - MSG).

Let's start exercising our power and right to remove sin by practicing to forgive. Release people from their sins. This is a great act of love, and love covers (or removes) a multitude of sins.

Above all, keep fervent in your love for one another, because love covers a multitude of sins. (1 Peter 4:8 - NASB).

Chapter 10

THE TRANSMUTATIONAL POWER OF THE BELIEVER

For this chapter, I want to zoom in on the Patriarch, Abraham. We know Abraham is considered the father of faith, the father of many nations, and a friend of God. There is just so much that is revealed in the life of Abraham by the canon, but there is so much more that was not included. Reading his story felt a little bit disjointed to me, so I was glad when I found the Apocalypse of Abraham.

According to Wikipedia, the first English translation of this book was released in 1898. Most believers have never even heard of this book. Thankfully, there are also audio versions on YouTube that you can listen to.

This book was a treat to read as it filled in a lot of the gaps we see in the canon Bible. I am a storyteller, so I know when snippets or details are missing from a story.

The Apocalypse of Abraham gave a backstory to the life of this Patriarch. It should help us better understand his journey and relationship with the Lord.

Abraham was a friend of God, and he was taken up to the seventh heaven. The Bible only speaks of a first and third heaven. Abraham apparently saw the beginning of time and the end of an age. What I am not sure about is whether Abraham saw the end of the age for his people or all mankind?

Abraham mentioned the age of the godless, and I think that is the age of the Gentiles. Gentiles are very ungodly people, not like the Jews. Even Jews who have not accepted that the Messiah has already come are still more godly than Gentiles. I am sure there are exceptions.

Paul talks about the age of the Gentiles in Romans 11:25:

For I do not want you, brothers and sisters, to be uninformed of this mystery—so that you will not be wise in your own estimation—that a partial hardening has happened to Israel until the fullness of the Gentiles has come in. (Romans 11:25 - NASB).

So there is a deliberate blindness where the Jews are concerned so Gentiles have a go at salvation. This is really an age of grace for God to extend such a beautiful opportunity for restoration to a savage group of people.

In Genesis 12, Abram is given an instruction to leave his home country to go somewhere—God doesn't say where. I was stoked at Abram's capacity to obey such an instruction without question, but my reservations were alleviated when I read the Apocalypse. Abraham wasn't born hearing the voice of God. This clarity came through desire and an earnest seeking after the true God. When

God spoke in Genesis 12, Abram had no reservations obeying because he knew God.

The promise that God would make him into a great nation was not news to Abram. God already told him when he took him up to heaven. This solved a lot of problems for me. I used to wonder how these Biblical writers spoke to God with such clarity. I know now they all went through the process of earnestly seeking God to get to that level.

There is more:

And Abram took Sarai his wife, and Lot his brother's son, and all their substance that they had gathered, and the souls that they had gotten in Haran; and they went forth to go into the land of Canaan; and into the land of Canaan they came. (Genesis 12:5 - KJV).

If you study the original text, this verse actually says **"...the souls they had made."**

When you win a soul, the soul becomes your responsibility. You are commissioned with making disciples of the soul you win. This is one area where tele-evangelists fail. They make souls but not disciples. The command from Jesus is to make disciples. Did you realize that is another way to say "make souls?"

There are two words I want you to take note of in Genesis 12:8, Mountain and Tent. These words are repeated throughout scripture, and it is not always in reference to the physical counterpart. Jesus went up into a mountain to pray. I have been told that there are no mountains in Jerusalem. I don't know if this is true or not.

141

Another thing to note is when people **"called upon the name of the Lord."** I am sure we all have that experience of calling "Jesus" and not getting a response or seeing a manifestation. So what did it mean for the Patriarchs back then? The name of the Lord was not the English word we use now "Jesus" because the letter "J" is pretty young in our English language. So, what name did they use? Why was this practice so powerful?

I mention all this so we know that if we accept the call to go higher in God and seek out the depths and mystery of the divine, we will understand experientially what many of the Biblical writers wrote about. The realities we perceive now and try to make work supernaturally are not the same realities they knew and manifested. They understood both worlds and tried to give language to a world we don't understand very well.

The Bible says everyone who calls upon the name of the Lord will be saved. Men have been calling on the name of the Lord since the days of Seth, so what is the name? I will leave this discussion open for another book. Let's get back to Abraham.

There was a famine in the land. Yet, in Genesis 13:2, it says Abraham was rich in cattle, silver, and gold. It means as children of God, we are not subjugated to the systems of this world. As believers, we live from a higher place. Unbelievers function under the sun, and there is nothing new under the sun. Believers are seated above the sun. Abraham was prospering in a time of famine.

Abraham lived in the time of Nimrod. If you see the name "Amraphel" anywhere in scripture, this is the same person. There were many nations at the time, but I believe the Biblical narrative focused on the lineage from which the Messiah would come. A war broke out between kings and Lot and all he owned were taken.

Remarkably, when Abraham got the news, he took 318 armed, trained souls/servant and pursued, rescued, and recovered all. There are millions of believers on earth, but you just need a few to answer a higher call to change the world. This is not something Abba forces on anyone. You are a god on the earth, so you can live your life any way you please…good or bad. Free will is a power not even God overrides, though I believe He can.

In Genesis 14:18-20, we see the first mention of Melchizedek. Here, we also see the only mention of a city called Salem in the Scriptures. These verses are interjected between two verses mentioning the king of Sodom coming to Abraham and asking a favour. We see two realities overlapping each other, which is always the case.

Who was Melchizedek?

For this Melchizedek, king of Salem, priest of the Most High God, who met Abraham returning from the slaughter of the kings and blessed him, to whom also Abraham gave a tenth part of all, first being translated "king of righteousness," and then also king of Salem, meaning "king of peace," without father, without mother, without genealogy, having neither beginning of days nor end of life, but made like the Son of God, remains a priest continually. (Hebrews 7:1-3 - NKJV).

Melchizedek appears to be a human being but a glorified one. Maybe he represents the future transfigured being that believers become, or maybe he is just one of his own kind. The Bible does support that when we became believers, we also became a priest after the order of Melchizedek, meaning the mortal genealogy and limitations no longer apply to us. Remember, **"No eye has seen, no ear has heard…"**

Abraham's life seemingly gets difficult when he and his wife agreed to produce an heir through their own efforts. Ishmael was born. The mother of Ishmael became arrogant. Sarai complained. Abraham sent Hagar away. An angel found her and sent her back.

As children of God, we should not run away from difficult circumstances. By facing it, we can change it into something good.

Abraham's life was very profound. We know he interceded for a city God was determined to destroy. I have heard that every number Abraham suggested had significance because he understood how the real world worked. The numbers Abraham mentioned are 50, 45, 40, 30, 20 and 10. I will say no more on that.

Abraham was a human being just like us, and all the other Biblical characters we have talked about and may mention going forward. They recorded their experience, not to awe the generations to follow, but to enlighten us to what we have access to. Additionally, by virtue of the finished work of Jesus Christ, we may just have access to even greater. This hardly resonates with people from my nation because we know Christianity from a purely religious perspective, not from a mystical/spiritual reality. We have grouped everything we can see as real; everyone who prays the sinner's prayer as saved, those who stopped going to church as backsliders, and anything supernatural or spiritual as demonic. It is a sad travesty that has locked us out of the true kingdom reality for centuries, and if one dares to break free and untether from the system of religion, he/she becomes an outcast.

God can be known—at least what He wants us to know—not by study, not by perception, not by what others think, but by God making Himself known to the one who has emptied him/herself of every false perception and is open to know the truth as Truth reveals Himself. The transmutational power of the believer is concealed within God Himself who determines the measure of release by relational interactions. There is no formula to walk in the supernatural because it flows out of God, who must be free to be Himself in the context of the one He embodies.

If you meet me as the author of this book for the first time, and you have no idea who I am, and you approach the meeting without judgment or preconception, you will get to experience me as I am. If you have some preconceived knowledge of who I am by what you have read or heard, then you will filter my revelation of myself to you through those lenses. If someone told you I get angry very easily, you will keep looking for that to manifest and may even interpret other emotional manifestations as anger. I may even say to you that I am not angry, and you will say I am lying. This is exactly why religion becomes a hindrance to actually knowing God, and this truncates our ability to manifest God as God desires to be manifested.

Every believer is guilty of saying no to God, thinking it is devils when it is not, and resisting God actually trying to reveal Himself as He chooses to.

Potentially, we have so much power by virtue of the One who indwells us, but it is our level of maturity that stops us from manifesting higher levels of spiritual influence. The substance that creates gold must first be tried by fire before it manifests its true form. The transmutational power of the believer is already there, but it can only be activated by maturity, and maturity comes by passing through the process that God allows.

Although He was a Son, He learned obedience from the things which He suffered. (Hebrews 5:8 - NKJV).

Chapter 11

THIEVES, KILLERS, ACCUSERS, LIARS, AND DESTROYERS SEEKING REFUGE

There is a kingdom inside us. The more I meditate on this, the more I realize that the first kingdom we are called to rule is us. The kingdom is not just inside us, but it is us, and we are tasked with the responsibility to govern and rule this kingdom first before we are qualified to rule nations and worlds.

Where many believers fail is in governing the kingdom that they are. The day has come when it is not acceptable for someone to project a saved, sanctified persona for the world to see, preaching and teaching the gospel, and even walking in a supernatural reality, when there are imposters living within their kingdom that cause them to err. We have seen a lot of this being brought into the spotlight, where famous preachers have been caught up in sexual-related scandals and all kinds of debauchery. Apparently, it is the struggle of many believers to battle their demons in seclusion and isolation, while perpetuating a holy persona. So many people struggle in different areas, but a lack of accountability and help may cause them to suppress their weak areas, keeping them in the dark. This is a terrible practice.

I want to demystify the myth that the thief spoken about in John 10 is this one powerful super being. It is not one but many.

Anything that comes opposing the life of God is a thief, and there are many.

When an unclean spirit goes out of a man, he goes through dry places, seeking rest; and finding none, he says, 'I will return to my house from which I came.' (Luke 11:24 - NKJV).

Sin was not in the original design of man. By disobedience, sin was allowed to enter this world, and sin then feeds on the water of man. If there is no water, sin entities cannot survive. It needs a dwelling place and seeks refuge in the temple we are building for God. All our struggles and eventual glory emanate from within. The greatest battle we have to fight is within—it is to evict all trespassers from God's house.

Let's be specific. For years I struggled with porn. It was a deep desire that welled up within me daily—a call I felt compelled to answer. We must understand how sin works from the beginning. Eve had a conversation with a serpent. Once she acted on that, sin entered and took up residence. It becomes easy to repeat that sin after the first act. The danger is not in the conversation but in taking action. If it is in acting we open ourselves to receive something that is not-God, then maybe it is in acting that we can expel it.

I want to use the beginning of Job's story to illustrate a point. It is not to say this is exactly how things transpired, but there is something we can glean from that story. We must be mindful that at every given moment, waves of energy and frequency emanate from our being that are tied to our thoughts, emotions, and will. We are creators, just like our Father. We are either exuding life or death; we are either creating life or death. Our ignorance of this reality has been detrimental to the world we live in. Remember, we were created to rule and govern creation. It means then that we can also be responsible for its destruction.

There was a man in the land of Uz, whose name was Job; and that man was perfect and upright, and one that feared God, and eschewed evil. (Job 1:1 - KJV).

The use of the word "perfect" in this text does not mean he was without error. It means his bloodline was pure and undefiled. The mixing of species is nothing new, and it will always be considered evil and lead to destruction. We see this with the flood and Sodom and Gomorrah.

And there were born unto him seven sons and three daughters. (Job 1:2 - KJV).

Job had ten children. This is a significant number repeated throughout scripture. In Hebrew culture, it is a sign of infinite possibilities with the 1 and the 0. In mathematics, IO is infinity.

We see 10 repeated throughout Job 1: 7000 sheep plus 3000 camels is 10,000; 500 oxen plus 500 asses is 1,000. If we understand Hebrew hieroglyphics and numbers, we understand how the spiritual dimension works. Job was very familiar with how to access spiritual realities.

Job was regarded as the greatest of all the men of the east. East is not just a direction but an access point. The mystical fathers teach that anything coming into this realm from other realms uses the east gate, which is why east is repetitive throughout scripture. Job knew how to access other realms.

And it was so, when the days of their feasting were gone about, that Job sent and sanctified them, and rose up early in the morning, and offered burnt offerings according to the number of them all: for Job said, it may be that my sons have sinned, and cursed God in their hearts. Thus did Job continually. (Job 1:5 - KJV).

If Job lived before Abraham, then the issue of burnt offerings and the sanctification and forgiveness that came with that had not yet been instituted. It means Job was drawing from a future reality, as did most, if not all, the Patriarchs. They saw a day that was coming and harvested from that in their present time. Job had prophetic insight. He knew how to secure sanctification for his children, just in case they had sinned.

Even today, occultists make sacrifices to access certain spiritual realities. How do they know to do that? What practice are they counterfeiting? What does the real practice look like today?

Now there was a day when the sons of God came to present themselves before the Lord, and Satan came also among them. (Job 1:6 - KJV).

Why is satan permitted to appear before the Lord? Is he not a fallen being? How could a fallen being be allowed to enter God's presence so freely? I am sure you have asked these questions as well. I would question the location of this meeting because no fallen angel can access heaven and be in the presence of God from my limited understanding.

The Lord proceeds to have a conversation about Job in the presence of the sons of God. What is interesting is that this same conversation is written elsewhere, but about Abram prior to him being tempted to offer his son as a sacrifice. Other writings say Abram was tempted ten times by the Lord; 10 tests, the final was with his son, Isaac. So here again we see the repetition of 10: ten plagues in Egypt, ten times spoken to create the world.

These "coincidences" point to the possibility that becoming mature and perfect as a son requires us to pass through these ten as well. The last test being giving up what is most dear to us. Do you see the similarity with Job? Was there anything more dear to him than his children?

Before Jesus came into the fullness of His ministry, He was taken into the wilderness by the Spirit to be tempted. I think that most Christians get stuck here failing these tests, which is why we have not yet emerged in the fullness of who we are. When God asked me to give up a friend I thought I couldn't live without, my answer was no. We all struggle with letting go of things we think we cannot live without, even our very lives. But maturity and operating in the power of God requires us to surrender all; a price most of us will not pay, but we still want the benefits. The power of the God of the universe cannot be handed down to immature children. It is also a heart issue because the heart is desperately wicked, according to Scripture, because that is where the serpent sits.

So the death to self is not a death to the true you, but a death to the serpent that is also you, so the real you can emerge. This is the process Job went through.

Who tempted Eve in the Garden? Who tempted Jesus? Who tempts you?

For if our heart condemns us, God is greater than our heart, and knows all things. (1 John 3:20 - NKJV).

Our heart becomes an adversary to us, and satan means adversary. Because of how we are built and the serpentine nature that now exists within us, we can project an accusatory version of ourselves, the serpentine version of self, that appears before God among the sons of God, which you are, that accuses and condemns you.

When you are tempted by this version of you, if you fail the test, you become that which tempted you. It is a fight for dominance. What would Jesus have become had He failed the tests in the wilderness? Thankfully, we don't have to find out.

We were made in the image and likeness of God; powerful beings that could rule and govern a creation that spans infinite light years. For sin to enter this equation, a fragmentation of self occurs beyond human comprehension. You think your life is small and insignificant, but you have no idea the effect you have on this world.

It is vital we go through tests and trials because it is the only way to face and defeat the serpent that is you so the true you can emerge.

Remember, Jesus called Peter "satan." He wasn't saying he was one of the fallen satans. Peter was projecting an adversary at that moment. So there are satans that fell, but there are satans that are a projection of you, and you must face and overcome these versions of yourself, or you become what you don't overcome.

Job lost everything. I used to think that Job was unaware of the conversation that seemingly took place behind his back, but watch what he says in Job 3:25:

For the thing I greatly feared has come upon me, and what I dreaded has happened to me. (Job 3:25 - NKJV).

Fear creates a reality we do not want. How does this work? By thought and imagining, we form a reality in our minds that plays out like a scene from a movie. This is how we create. Eventually, those scenes play out in real life. Could the scene we read in Job 1 be a creation of Job's fears? If that is the case, can we say God directly gave permission to satan to inflict Job?

Do you realize that by your thoughts, imagination, and speech, you are creating realities in the realm of the unseen that you must eventually face and overcome? Every thought, good or bad, wants to become real and seeks a kingdom to dwell and manifest in. If you don't understand your significance in this world, you become a vessel through which all kinds of negative energies manifest themselves.

When you overcome these experiences that you create, you disempower or kill that version of you that created that reality and wanted to become you. This is why we must see every challenge and test as something to overcome. The moment you accept or allow a thief and robber or any other temporary energy to define your reality, you give power to a false version of yourself.

Job's experience was created by fear. Anything we create from fear must be destroyed in order to emerge as our true selves. Fear has existed from the very beginning when man fell.

So he said, "I heard Your voice in the garden, and I was afraid because I was naked; and I hid myself." (Genesis 3:10 - NKJV).

Immediately after the fall, man started to create false realities that became their experiences. Thus, the ego was born, and the nature of the ego is fear. The difficulties you face now are not designed to destroy the real you, just the false versions of yourself that you created. It is your responsibility to rule the kingdom that you are. You are the king and priest, the lord and god, and the gatekeeper of your kingdom.

There are versions of you that are an adversary to your true self. This is the conflict that exists within every believer. In Job's case, and ours, God's response to the adversary is what is important. God basically says, "You don't know him like I do."

There is something about God that baffles me. He will allow every single human being on earth the freedom to decide who they are, and who He is. So now there are so many variations of the knowledge of God on earth that one has to wonder if the true and living God is in any of it. I have read so many stories and seen so many variations of God and self, and so many of them are rooted in our experiences of the world. Everything wrong with our world today originated from man. Instead of taking responsibility, we are always looking for someone to blame. The devil got most of it.

So, someone asked, "How can a good God sit in heaven and allow bad things to happen to good people on earth?" The same can be said about you. Didn't Jesus say to whom the Word of God has come, ye are gods (see John 10:34-36). So, how does a good god sit on the earth and allow bad things to happen to good people? Aren't you a son of God? Are you a bad god to allow bad things to happen to good people? Would you give your life to save the life of another human being?

Can a son blame his Father if he is a poor steward of his own inheritance?

Job's conversations with himself and his friends was a blame game: Who is responsible?

The origin of our troubles is not necessarily demonic. Take a lesson from Job. We or our friends are not as qualified to speak to our true value or God's nature and character because we filter our perception through our circumstances. Your value is not skewed or determined by what you are going through. God's character or your true self is not defined by your earthly experiences. God is the only one qualified to represent Himself and represent the true you.

Many of our experiences today are rooted in what other people have spoken or what we ourselves have spoken. Was God doing anything to Job? No, He wasn't. Job went to war with his own fears that created a traumatic reality that neither he nor his friends could comprehend.

I grew up in church where the language of self is how bad and wretched we are. Those are accusations from our false selves that we believed, thus cementing their reality and shaping our identity. We didn't form our identity growing up by what God said about us or the value He placed on us. We assumed our worth on the merit of the false accusations against us. As such, we must now go to war with self if we are ever going to emerge in the fulness of who God created us to be. The Bible says He is Lord of lords and King of kings. It is funny how we exclude ourselves from being lords and kings and accept a more filthy disposition.

We must begin to rid our kingdom of these imposters who want to become us but are not. They are temporary, ugly trespassers seeking refuge in God's temple. They are of our own creation, and it is in our power and ability to annihilate them so the son of God that we are can manifest unhindered and unfiltered.

Chapter 12

LIVING THE ASCENDED LIFE

When Adam fell, man was no longer a fully manifested human being but a fallen version of himself. This is the context in which we know a human being. We hardly have a clue as it relates to our original estate or how we function, which is why man is the greatest mystery on earth that even angels are flabbergasted at our existence.

In order for creation not to exercise superiority over man, creation itself was supressed.

For the creation was subjected to frustration and futility, not willingly [because of some intentional fault on its part], but by the will of Him who subjected it, in hope that the creation itself will also be freed from its bondage to decay [and gain entrance] into the glorious freedom of the children of God. (Romans 8:20-21 - AMP).

Creation has not responded to a human being the way it did to Adam before the fall, until Jesus Christ came. Here we have the second Adam, who was now a fully manifested human being, though fully God. The Bible is clear that His identity and divinity are our inheritance, for we are:

- Joint heirs with Him (see Romans 8:17).

- Sons adopted into the family of God (see Ephesians 1:5).

As He is, so are we (see 1 John 4:17). This is where it gets mind-boggling as we think we are too wretched to put ourselves in the same sentence as Jesus. We don't do it, but He does. This is why without faith, it is impossible to please God. The quintessential issue of faith is actually believing what God says when our fallen nature is screaming to the contrary. Let's explore this some more.

- Jesus is fully God, now fully man. In the words of my mentor, "There is a man in the Godhead."

- The first Adam is no more.

- Human beings are a fallen race.

Jesus, as the second Adam, is the full embodiment of what God had in mind when He made man. Several things happen at the moment of conversion:

1. **We are made into a new creation (see 2 Corinthians 5:17). New means never existed before, so there really is no reference for this. I believe the full revelation of who we are is revealed but still hidden.**

It is not that we have received a new body. Our body is still awaiting its full redemption, so what part of us is truly new? It must then be a new spirit or soul, and since spirit is really the breath of God, and God is Spirit, so it doesn't require renewal, then what is left to be made new must be the soul.

2. We are seated with Christ in heavenly places.

Here we see Jesus' declaration that where He is, we will also be. This multi-dimensional reality of which we are engrafted is frowned upon because of our perceived limitation of our unredeemed bodies. We must be mindful that the limitations of the body are not the limitations of our soul. We are seated with Christ, so wherever He is, we are there.

3. We are given access to all things pertaining to life and godliness (see 2 Peter 1:3).

All things mean nothing left out, nothing broken, nothing lacking. All that we were, are, and are becoming is already inside us. The future is simply the unravelling of the true man in God. The deeper we get into the depth of God is the more we become. It is impossible for religion or any other system to take us to where God wants to take us.

4. We are given the Holy Spirit.

This is the same Spirit who hovered over chaos and brought order in the beginning, manifesting creation and new creations. There is no force in all existence more powerful than the Holy Spirit, who is God. For the most part, we have limited His true function in our lives, which is something God seems to allow. I don't understand why.

Now here is one of the most beautiful texts of scripture:

Jesus answered, "If anyone [really] loves Me, he will keep My word (teaching); and My Father will love him, and We will

come to him and make Our dwelling place with him." (John
14:23) - AMP).

If it is true that a vessel is defined by what it is filled with, then
when God makes His dwelling in us, what does that truly mean?

As a new soul, seated with Christ, embedded into the Godhead,
having access to the fullness of God, we have all power, all
authority, and all things because we are the home of God. This is
where He lives. If God dwells in heaven, it means heaven,
somehow, is also within the believer.

He has made everything beautiful in its time. Also He has put
eternity in their hearts, except that no one can find out the
work that God does from beginning to end. (Ecclesiastes 3:11
- NKJV).

We have become an eternal dwelling place for God. The fullness
of the Godhead now dwells in the follower of Christ. So now we
begin to understand Jesus' prayer in John 17. There is a oneness
that exists between the believer and God. There is no separation,
so we are now called to live an ascended life, as Jesus did.

The problem in human history is that there are those who want to
be god independent of God. This is a self-generated false version
of self that we create by virtue of the fall, and it is referred to as
the ego or self. The ego or self is false and has no eternal
inheritance whatsoever. It dies when the human being dies, and
there is no resurrection for it. In order to achieve the abundant
life Jesus spoke about in John 10:10. The ego or self must die
while we live.

> **Then He said to them all, "If anyone desires to come after Me, let him deny himself, and take up his cross daily, and follow Me." (Luke 9:23 - NKJV).**

The self is everybody's problem. Its voice is loud; it often conceals itself as the voice of God and is attached to everything we want to do wrong that God advises us to flee from. It also forces us to remain earthbound and deny our true identity. We cannot manifest God through self because self is not connected to God, nor can it be. Self is our own creation (because we are creators), and only we can destroy it and strip it of its influential powers. It is this struggle why most believers may never experience the fullness of who they are until they die. The one who desires to be god without God will fall. That was Eve's downfall.

> **For you have said in your heart: 'I will ascend into heaven, I will exalt my throne above the stars of God; I will also sit on the mount of the congregation on the farthest sides of the north; I will ascend above the heights of the clouds, I will be like the Most High.' (Isaiah 14:13-14 - NKJV).**

The king of Babylon spoke these words. This is the ultimate outworking of the god-complex that we see operating even in churches. Leaders want to be served and elevated on pedestals when they are called to be servants.

Being god is about being in union with God, and this union is a reality yet to be embraced by most believers. The ego must be addressed if we are to walk in the fullness of this "oneness" reality.

Many believers, including myself, are living out of our false selves instead of our true selves. Most don't even know there is a difference. The real war within is between the false self and the new soul. Both are us. The dominant one is the one we allow to influence our decisions, thought processes, belief systems, and how we process information.

The will empowers both the new soul and the false self. So the will is independent of the soul and not a make-up of it, as often postulated by church doctrine. Every time we say "I will, I can, I can't, I am," we are either talking from the false self or the true self. This is why affirmations are so important in cementing who we truly are.

So how do we live this ascended life? I want to take the time to briefly examine some of the practical spiritual practices or disciplines we must adapt for spiritual transformation. There are no alternatives, so if any of these are rejected because people use them falsely, it is to your own peril.

I want to over-emphasize the prayer in John 17. It is one of the most powerful prayers recorded in Scripture, and I hardly hear anyone preach or teach on it. As a matter of fact, the idea of oneness with God is seemingly taboo. It is inconceivable, and maybe even impossible, but is it?

Here is a possibility: Most of our theology was developed by people who never learned to master sin, which means their inability to match up to what is believed to be holiness is embedded in our theology. If you don't believe mastering sin is possible, you will never believe in the possibility of union with God.

We have tried to control sin by enforcing rules, and this has not worked for even the enforcers of these rules. There are more doctrines of men and devils than there are doctrines of God. Research has proven that you cannot modify a person's behaviour long-term with rules and punishment. They will always try to find a way to circumvent the rules to do what they want to do.

Let's say, for example, fornication is what I want to do, but the new creation that I am says don't do it. Then I would have to cut myself off from creating the possibility by avoiding being with someone somewhere for it to happen. Yet, the reality is, I really want to do this thing. As we discuss spiritual disciplines in living the ascended life, this is the conflict we all must face. The challenge is, how do we grow or mature our souls enough to not want to do this thing, even if we are put in a position like Joseph was? Even David failed initially, but eventually, he got a handle on it. The struggle is real.

We are given spiritual practices and disciplines that, if done right, will mature the soul. I believe the born again experience and the Christian journey have to do with the soul. Remember, in the beginning, Adam was made a living soul. So now the Bible says:

Beloved, I pray that you may prosper in all things and be in health, just as your soul prospers. (3 John 1:2 - NKJV).

Health and prosperity are intricately tied to the health and prosperity of the soul. So spiritual practices are for the soul. All spiritual practice must be approached from a place of oneness; otherwise, it becomes dead works with very little to no benefit to the practitioner.

The first spiritual discipline is worship.

God is Spirit, and those who worship Him must worship in spirit and truth. (John 4:24 - NKJV).

God is Spirit. Some translations add "a," but most translations say God is Spirit, and those who worship Him must worship Him in Spirit and Truth. If God is Spirit, then Spirit is God, and there really are no other spirits per se because God is omnipresent. To worship God in Spirit and as spirit is to understand that we are not separated from Him anymore.

Worship leaders love when people obey and respond to them, but that is vain and egotistical. We really don't need to do anything with our physical body to worship because worship is something we become, not something we do. The journey of faith is one of becoming, not doing.

Worship must be genuine, not co-hersed. It must be authentic. It doesn't mean we should be lazy with our bodies. The outer must be a reflection of the inner. True worship is done in Spirit and truth, not pretense and not putting on a show.

The second spiritual discipline is prayer.

But you, when you pray, go into your room, and when you have shut your door, pray to your Father who is in the secret place; and your Father who sees in secret will reward you openly. (Matthew 6:6 - NKJV).

Prayer was never meant to be a public thing. What goes public is the fruit of a prayer life. No one eats from the roots of a tree; they always reach for the fruit. Jesus even told us what not to do when we pray:

And when you pray, you shall not be like the hypocrites. For they love to pray standing in the synagogues and on the corners of the streets, that they may be seen by men. Assuredly, I say to you, they have their reward. (Matthew 6:5 - NKJV).

The only reward for such prayers is to be lauded by men, which really has no eternal value whatsoever. A study of Moses' Tabernacle reveals some similarities with our bodies. There is the outer court, the inner court, and the holy of holies. The priest would go into the holy of holies and minister to God, then come out and minister to the people. We must learn to pray from this inner chamber within the fabric of our being because that is where God dwells. David calls it the "Secret Place."

He who dwells in the secret place of the Most High Shall abide under the shadow of the Almighty. (Psalm 91:1 - NKJV).

Think of another occasion where *shadow* is mentioned in scripture, and you will begin to understand how powerful this is. If we don't learn to pray from the holy of holies, our ministry cannot be as effective as it should be.

Here is something else with prayer:

Likewise the Spirit also helps in our weaknesses. For we do not know what we should pray for as we ought, but the Spirit Himself makes intercession for us with groanings which cannot be uttered. (Romans 8:26 - NKJV).

Spirit is God, so we worship Spirit as spirit, and we also pray as Spirit. This is God talking to God. So prayer is self-talk between God and Himself, and in the words of my mentor, if God talks to Himself, He will answer Himself.

But you, beloved, building yourselves up on your most holy faith, praying in the Holy Spirit. (Jude 1:20 - NKJV).

Prayer is not about trying to get God to do something for us. It is a willingness to participate in what God is doing. For example, if we pray for there to be more love in the world, we must be willing to become that love. In other words, for the prayer we pray to be effective, we must be willing to be the answer to the prayer as well. Keep in mind as well that every thought is a prayer to God.

The third spiritual discipline is fellowship.

Not forsaking the assembling of ourselves together, as is the manner of some, but exhorting one another, and so much the more as you see the Day approaching. (Hebrews 10:25 - NKJV).

We have used this verse to create cults to the detriment of families. So many wives, husbands, fathers, and mothers forsake their family and friends for church.

If we should look at this verse in context, it speaks to the idea of our internal structure as the temple of God. When we begin to spend time with God in the secret place, the temptation becomes isolation. The author is saying, don't do that.

A priest goes into the holy of holies alone, then comes out to minister to people and fellowship. When we have been with God, we want to be with people…family first, then others. As a matter of fact, the foundation of the church gathering should be families.

Also, let's consider this verse:

For where two or three are gathered together in My name, I am there in the midst of them. (Matthew 18:20 - NKJV).

You don't need a mega-church setting for Jesus to show up. You also don't need the theatrics we often engage in, claiming to attract the presence of God. We will soon see that the use of the word "in" denotes a location and nothing else.

The final spiritual discipline I want to touch on is meditation.

Every sect practices meditation, except Christianity. Meditation is a means of accessing the spiritual realm. You cannot fall into a trance or have altered states of consciousness unless you meditate.

I don't know anyone who practices meditation who does not have spiritual experiences. I don't know anyone who does not practice meditation who has spiritual experiences. Again, the language of the Bible is interesting:

I will meditate in thy precepts, and have respect unto thy ways. (Psalm 119:15 - KJV).

My hands also will I lift up unto thy commandments, which I have loved; and I will meditate in thy statutes. (Psalm 119:48 - KJV).

Let the proud be ashamed; for they dealt perversely with me without a cause: but I will meditate in thy precepts. (Psalm 119:78 - KJV).

Do you see the constant use of the word "in?" If you miss that one little word, you miss a lot. In the beginning, for example, is a location in God, not an event. "In the name" is also a location. We must locate ourselves "in," or we will have the same experience with God asking us the question as He did Adam and Job "Where are you?" or 'Where were you?"

Spiritual laws were established by God at creation. These laws have not changed. What has changed is how they have been used. Fallen man can create derivatives of these laws, but the principle remains the same. New Agers, for example, use meditation, but meditation is not New Age. New Agers chant, but chanting is not New Age. As a matter of fact, the name of God is often used by these people to gain access because there is no other name to use.

Meditation, when done the right way, brings quietness to our beings, almost taking us to a place where there is nothing. You cannot talk about living the ascended life by excluding this practice. In that place of nothingness, there is no doctrine, no beliefs, no images, no pre-conceived ideas of God or reality. It is a pure place from which all things emerged that form a part of our reality today. This is actually the purest place to be, and this is where God is purely and from where God will do a new thing.

Be still, and know that I am God: I will be exalted among the heathen, I will be exalted in the earth. (Psalm 46:10 - KJV).

There is a knowing that can only be experienced in stillness. At a place of "no-thing" you can access everything.

Chapter 13

AS HE IS

...without father, without mother, without genealogy, having neither beginning of days nor end of life, but made like the Son of God, remains a priest continually. (Hebrews 7:3 - NKJV).

This is a description of Melchizedek, but it is also a description of man in his original form. The issue I have with knowing this is that it seems like most of humanity have lost their way. They have no inclination about who they are, and to some extent, they couldn't care less. Thank God this is not you. If you have read through this book to this point, I sense your hunger, and I will ensure you are properly fed in this chapter because it is about you, the true you.

You are a child of God born from eternity. When you were born again, or born from above, the new you had to pass through every sphere and dimension from here all the way into the depths of God where you were birth when you said yes to Jesus. In other words, your DNA is imprinted in all dimensions, giving you access to it all.

> **Love has been perfected among us in this: that we may have boldness in the day of judgment; because as He is, so are we in this world. (1 John 4:17 - NKJV).**

I know you are ready for this or you wouldn't be reading this book.

We are like Jesus more than we know.

Jesus asked a question. **"What will it profit a man to gain the whole world and lose his soul?"** Or **"What can a man give in exchange for his soul?"** If you are wondering about your value, Jesus told you. One soul is of equal value to the "whole world." It means the soul that doesn't accept Jesus will lose its first estate or eternal inheritance.

The first time we came into existence was in the mind of God. He saw us, spoke to us, and engaged us long before the world was created. That is why the Bible says we were chosen before the foundation of the world because we were already real to God (see Ephesians 1:4-6). There is a pre-determined path for every human being to come into their original estate, which can only be accessed through faith in Yeshua Hamashiach (Jesus, the Christ.) There is no other way. You can access fragmented and lower frequencies because you are a human being, but you can never come into the fullness of who you are outside of Christ. The issue of being gods is that we are gods inside the true and living God. It is by virtue of union where God decided to share His divinity with created man. The level at which God shares is to give you full access to all that He is. According to 1 John 4:17, whatever is true about Jesus is also true about you.

> **For in Him dwells all the fullness of the Godhead bodily; and you are complete in Him, who is the head of all principality and power. (Colossians 2:9-10 - NKJV).**

For the believer, there is no partial indwelling of God. It doesn't make you Him, but it makes you like Him.

There is a process that we go through to come into maturity. Let's say, drawing from scripture and other materials, that there are ten levels of testing that the child of God must go through to come into sonship. If there are ten levels, then there are ten dimensions of growth, and each dimension has its own protocols. It means then that what works to get you through one level becomes irrelevant when you get to the next. This is also true when it comes to the close of one age and the beginning of the next. The church is losing relevance because we entered a new age and are still using the same protocols from the age that closed. But this is not what we are talking about.

Jesus had to move through these different levels as well. The first thing we see is Him being taken into the wilderness to be tested.

> **Then Jesus was led up by the Spirit into the wilderness to be tempted by the devil. (Matthew 4:1 - NKJV).**

It is the Spirit that took Jesus into the wilderness almost immediately after He was baptised and the Father affirmed His position as a Son.

There are other Biblical writers who had their moments in the wilderness, so it is safe to say this is one level of testing. How well do we do in our wilderness moments? Is it a test we continue to fail? How do we fail the test? Do we fail the same way the children of Israel failed while going through their wilderness?

Then the Lord said: "I have pardoned, according to your word; but truly, as I live, all the earth shall be filled with the glory of the Lord—because all these men who have seen My glory and the signs which I did in Egypt and in the wilderness, and have put Me to the test now these ten times, and have not heeded My voice, they certainly shall not see the land of which I swore to their fathers, nor shall any of those who rejected Me see it." (Numbers 14:20-23 - NKJV).

Instead of passing the test, they turned around and tested God through their constant ingratitude, complaining, and grumbling.

As our journey to maturity continues, we must be mindful that God sees the bigger picture. He may allow us to go through fires, floods, storms, and many other maladies. They are not designed to destroy us but to shift us, but the shifting is incumbent on our response.

Do all things without complaining and disputing, that you may become blameless and harmless, children of God without fault in the midst of a crooked and perverse generation, among whom you shine as lights in the world. (Philippians 2:14-15 - NKJV).

One of the tell-tale signs of immaturity in a believer is their constant bickering when things are not going well. We want to go back to what it was—our Egypt of sorts—because the new thing God is doing requires too much effort. We like things the way they are, and we don't want anything to change.

Jesus had to study, learn, experience, suffer, face temptations; the whole gamut. Jesus never came to relieve you of the work but to show you the path you must take for absolution.

After the fall of man, and the continuing fall, there was knowledge on the earth that eventually became lost. One such knowledge is who we are as human beings. If Jesus did not come, we, in this epoch, would have no idea what the original man was like before he sinned. We would forever embrace a reality based on the fallen context of man and not the original design. Today, I believe God is restoring a lot of knowledge that we have lost.

Jesus became a priest after the order of Melchizedek. It is the path for every believer. Melchizedek occupied an office outside of time in a city that was not in this dimension. When Abraham met him, Abraham paid tithes and had communion before any of these things were officially initiated on the earth. It means as a believer, we have access to a future not yet established on earth. This is what Hebrews talks about when it says **"partaking of the powers of the world to come."** How do you think the new heavens and the new earth are going to be established? Your doctrine says God will destroy this old earth and these old bodies and make new ones. If that was God's plan, He would have done it a long time ago. Why do you think creation groans and waits for the sons to manifest? What are they waiting for us to manifest? It is the new world locked in our DNA that is suppressed by the Babylonian systems of this world, including religion. Man creates systems to function on earth independent of God. Man wants to lock God out by controlling man so the God-man never emerges.

You have insight into a world without time, space, or matter where all that will ever be accomplished in creation is already a reality for God. Time carries us swiftly to the culmination of all things, but are we manifesting anything? Can we see a need the world is going to have a few years from now and establish a business in the present that will meet that need? Jesus was all this and so much more. So are you.

For it is evident that our Lord arose from Judah, of which tribe Moses spoke nothing concerning priesthood. And it is yet far more evident if, in the likeness of Melchizedek, there arises another priest who has come, not according to the law of a fleshly commandment, but according to the power of an endless life. (Hebrews 7:14-16 - NKJV).

Your priesthood and kingship are established according to the power of an endless life.

But He, because He continues forever, has an unchangeable priesthood. Therefore He is also able to save to the uttermost those who come to God through Him, since He always lives to make intercession for them. For such a High Priest was fitting for us, who is holy, harmless, undefiled, separate from sinners, and has become higher than the heavens; who does not need daily, as those high priests, to offer up sacrifices, first for His own sins and then for the people's, for this He did once for all when He offered up Himself. For the law appoints as high priests men who have weakness, but the word of the oath, which came after the law, appoints the Son who has been perfected forever. (Hebrews 7:24-28 - NKJV).

The road before us is not an easy one. For now, there is a conflict of will that affects the potency of our faith. There is "our will" which we will put up a pretty decent fight to hang on to, but there is "His will." In order to be counted among the chosen to establish the new heaven and earth or **"on earth as it is in heaven,"** we must walk the same path Jesus walked. There can only be "One will," which I will call "Your will" (not yours, but His.)

The Lord's prayer says **"Your will be done."** This is what we see Jesus do in the Garden of Gethsemane… **"Not my will, but Your will be done."** A failure to do this led to the fall of man in the beginning. Man still falls today because they are struggling to do this. What led to the fall of the son of the morning?

"How you are fallen from heaven, O Lucifer, son of the morning! How you are cut down to the ground, you who weakened the nations! For you have said in your heart: 'I will ascend into heaven, I will exalt my throne above the stars of God; I will also sit on the mount of the congregation on the farthest sides of the north; I will ascend above the heights of the clouds, I will be like the Most High.' Yet you shall be brought down to Sheol, to the lowest depths of the Pit. "Those who see you will gaze at you, and consider you, saying: 'Is this the man who made the earth tremble, who shook kingdoms, who made the world as a wilderness and destroyed its cities, who did not open the house of his prisoners?' (Isaiah 14:12-17 - NKJV).

There was no surrender of "my will." In order to be the god that God created you to be, there must be a surrender of your will to His. The most dangerous people on earth are gods with

unsurrendered wills, and they exist even in the church. The path
for a matured son includes the merging of wills, so all that
remains relevant is "Your (God's) will."

It is the will of God that must prevail in the life of the believer,
not the will of man. Gods have the power to make and enforce
laws and create systems of control that we become slaves to. We
are told how to dress, how to speak, how to act, when to act, what
to do and not do, and the true liberty that Holy Spirit brings is
lost or suppressed. Everyone thinks they are right and everyone
else is wrong, but the truth is, everyone is right, and everyone is
wrong.

**For now we see in a mirror, dimly, but then face to face. Now
I know in part, but then I shall know just as I also am known.
(1 Corinthians 13:12 - NKJV).**

Our walk with the Lord will differ from person to person, and as
God makes Himself known to each man/woman who decides to
walk with Him.

Hebrews 11 lists the heroes of faith: Abel, Enoch, Noah,
Abraham, Sarah, Isaac, Jacob, Joseph, Moses, Rahab, Joshua,
Gideon, Barak, Samson, Jephthah, David, and Samuel; they all
had a different story, but they did have one thing in common:
they saw the future.

**These all died in faith, not having received the promises, but
having seen them afar off were assured of them, embraced
them and confessed that they were strangers and pilgrims on
the earth. For those who say such things declare plainly that
they seek a homeland. And truly if they had called to mind**

that country from which they had come out, they would have had opportunity to return. But now they desire a better, that is, a heavenly country. Therefore God is not ashamed to be called their God, for He has prepared a city for them. (Hebrews 13:16 - NKJV).

We have received both the promise and the fulfillment, but our destinies are still tied with those who have gone before us:

And all these, having obtained a good testimony through faith, did not receive the promise, God having provided something better for us, that they should not be made perfect apart from us. (Hebrews 11:39 - NKJV).

What they saw and embraced by faith, we are living its reality: we have been engrafted into Christ, and there is no distinction or separation. This is the Good News for humanity and the reason why we witness so others can come into the fullness of who God created them to be, through Jesus Christ, our Lord, Saviour and Master.

Chapter 14

KEY TO IMMORTALITY

I don't believe there is just one key to immortality, but several keys. The starting point is to know it is possible to change from mortal to immortality without dying physically. This is not to say we won't die, but death is more optional than we think when it comes to the purposes and plans of God.

In this final chapter, we will be meditating and discussing one key. Let me first quote this key text in two different translations:

So then, brethren, we are debtors, but not to the flesh [we are not obligated to our carnal nature], to live [a life ruled by the standards set up by the dictates] of the flesh. For <u>if you live according to [the dictates of] the flesh, you will surely die.</u> But <u>if through the power of the [Holy] Spirit you are [habitually] putting to death (making extinct, deadening) the [evil] deeds prompted by the body, you shall [really and genuinely] live forever.</u> For all who are led by the Spirit of God are sons of God. For [the Spirit which] you have now received [is] not a spirit of slavery to put you once more in bondage to fear, but you have received the Spirit of adoption [the Spirit producing sonship] in [the bliss of] which we cry, Abba (Father)! Father! The Spirit Himself [thus] testifies together with our own spirit, [assuring us] that we are children of God. And if we are [His] children, then we are [His] heirs also: heirs of God and fellow heirs with Christ [sharing His inheritance with Him]; only we must share His suffering if we are to share His glory. (Romans 8:12-17 - AMPC).

Therefore, brethren, we are debtors—not to the flesh, to live according to the flesh. For if you live according to the flesh you will die; but <u>if by the Spirit you put to death the deeds of the body, you will live.</u> For as many as are led by the Spirit of God, these are sons of God. For you did not receive the spirit of bondage again to fear, but you received the Spirit of adoption by whom we cry out, "Abba, Father." The Spirit Himself bears witness with our spirit that we are children of God, and if children, then heirs—heirs of God and joint heirs with Christ, if indeed we suffer with Him, that we may also be glorified together. (Romans 8:12-17 - NKJV).

Herein lies one key to immortality: **putting to death the works of the flesh or the deeds of the body**, depending on which translation you are reading.

Since we are at the end of this book, and I imagine that only those whom this book is for would have made it to this point, let me be bold enough to make this statement: **If you can overcome in this area—put to death the works of the flesh—it will be nearly impossible for you to die a physical death.**

So, let us define what the works of the flesh are:

Now the works of the flesh are evident, which are: adultery, fornication, uncleanness, lewdness, idolatry, sorcery, hatred, contentions, jealousies, outbursts of wrath, selfish ambitions, dissensions, heresies, envy, murders, drunkenness, revelries, and the like; of which I tell you beforehand, just as I also told you in time past, that those who practice such things will not inherit the kingdom of God. (Galatians 5:19-21 – NKJV).

Let's extract a list. The works of the flesh are:

1. Adultery
2. Fornication
3. Uncleanness
4. Lewdness
5. Idolatry
6. Sorcery
7. Hatred
8. Contentions
9. Jealousies
10. Outburst of wrath
11. Selfish ambitions
12. Dissensions
13. Heresies
14. Envy
15. Murders
16. Drunkenness
17. Revelries

Take a few moments and meditate on this list. Can you honestly say that none of these things are an issue for you? At a glance, we may not even know what some of these things are. So, let's examine another translation:

> The wrong things the sinful self does are clear: <u>committing sexual sin</u>, <u>being morally bad</u>, <u>doing all kinds of shameful things</u>, <u>worshiping false gods</u>, <u>taking part in witchcraft</u>, <u>hating people</u>, <u>causing trouble</u>, <u>being jealous, angry or selfish</u>, <u>causing people to argue and divide into separate groups</u>, <u>being filled with envy</u>, <u>getting drunk</u>, <u>having wild parties</u>, and doing other things like this. I warn you now as I warned you before: The people who do these things will not have a part in God's kingdom. (Galatians 5:19-21 - ETRV).

Let me be candid and quite Biblical. If you do these things, you are not condemned.

> Therefore, there is no longer any condemnation awaiting those who are in union with the Messiah Yeshua. (Romans 8:1 - CJB).

Forgiveness is available for the son of God who sins.

> My children, I am writing you these things so that you won't sin. but if anyone does sin, we have Yeshua the Messiah, the Tzaddik, who pleads our cause with the Father. Also, he is the kapparah for our sins — and not only for ours, but also for those of the whole world. (1 John 2:1-2 - CJB).

So, you are not condemned, and you will be forgiven, but you will die. One way to transition from this life to the next without passing through the jaws of death is to overcome the works of the flesh. I believe this is why Elijah and Enoch could not die. I also believe this is the narrow way that only a few find.

Go in through the narrow gate; for the gate that leads to destruction is wide and the road broad, and many travel it; but it is a narrow gate and a hard road that leads to <u>life</u>, and only a few find it. (Matthew 7:13-14 - CJB).

Travelling the path to destruction doesn't necessarily mean you are on your way to hell. It means the path you take is destructive; for example, eating processed foods is destructive to your body. Lack of exercise is also destructive. Not maintaining a good mental health or engaging in spiritual practices are all destructive. You will die and go to heaven, but you have taken a destructive path that caused you to leave way before your time.

But how do we overcome the works of the flesh? After listing the works of the flesh, Apostle Paul continues:

But the fruit of the Spirit is love, joy, peace, patience, kindness, goodness, faithfulness, humility, self control. Nothing in the Torah stands against such things. Moreover, those who belong to the Messiah Yeshua have put their old nature to death on the stake, along with its passions and desires. Since it is through the Spirit that we have Life, let it also be through the Spirit that we order our lives day by day. Let us not become conceited, provoking and envying each other. (Galatians 5:22-26 - CJB).

There are two forces at work within the body of the believer; **the works of the flesh and the fruit of the Spirit.** One leads to death; the other leads to life. Every choice we make will be influenced by one or the other. I also want you to take note that it is your responsibility to put to death on the stake your old nature, not God's. "…**those who belong to the Messiah Yeshua**

have put their old nature to death on the stake, along with its passions and desires." God helps you by giving you His Spirit. By the Spirit, we can achieve the impossible, but the task is yours.

As a married man, whose wife works and travel, the temptation to partake in sexual sins is an issue. There is the issue of adultery, masturbation and pornography; issues that many struggle with silently. I am a pretty transparent person before God and man. I don't pretend to be who I'm not. So I often consider my own struggles, and it puzzles me. How can a desire for something—like another woman—be so strong, feel so good wanting it, yet be so wrong and destructive? Masturbation provides a release that calms the libido for a little bit. Even science is reporting that it is good for your health. So, how can this be destructive when it feels so natural?

This is the reality of our struggle with the works of the flesh. The desires feel like our own, and often, the conscience remains silent until an act is committed. This is the way that seems right to a man but leads to death.

Finally, Paul says those who take part in the works of the flesh will not have a part in God's kingdom. Some translations say you **"...will not inherit the kingdom of God."** We often interpret this to mean you are going to hell. The kingdom of God is the reality of heaven manifested on the earth. It is not the heaven we go to when we die. It is our capacity to manifest God's kingdom on the earth. This is why many who are sick have a greater chance of getting healed if they are prayed for by a monk than some who hold high offices in the church. Our failure to put to death the works of the flesh renders us powerless in manifesting the kingdom of God. We must choose which internal force we wish to empower. We cannot have it both ways. Each time we are faced with the decision to indulge in those things that are not-God, we are faced with a choice between death and life.

I call heaven and earth as witnesses today against you, that I have set before you life and death, blessing and cursing; therefore choose life, that both you and your descendants may live; that you may love the Lord your God, that you may obey His voice, and that you may cling to Him, for He is your life and the length of your days; and that you may dwell in the land which the Lord swore to your fathers, to Abraham, Isaac, and Jacob, to give them. (Deuteronomy 30:19-20 - NKJV).

Many believers are faced with this choice every day. Choose life.

CONCLUSION

The future is bright, glorious, and filled with unlimited possibilities. The ensuing chaos around us today will not compare to what will be revealed in and through the children of God. Our focus should be on what we want to manifest and what we want to multiply on the earth. Focusing on distractions will only multiply the chaos.

The world as we know it came out of man: the cars, planes, gadgets, medicines, you name it, it came out of fallen man. It means any possibility of any world to come must already be in man. I believe the new world (new earth) is embedded in the DNA of the children of God. Believers carry the potential for a better world, more specifically, a new heaven and a new earth. The reality of this was already created and placed inside the believer for future manifestation. This is what creation awaits. Creation is not groaning for the second coming of Christ but the revealing, evolution and, ultimately, the ascension of the sons of God.

Christianity was meant to be rooted in the reality of the incarnation: God becoming man; God becoming you. The paradox of our discussion is: God is you, but you are not God. You are a child of God—a son.

Behold what manner of love the Father has bestowed on us, that we should be called children of God! Therefore the world does not know us, because it did not know Him.

Beloved, now we are children of God; and it has not yet been revealed what we shall be, but we know that when He is revealed, we shall be like Him, for we shall see Him as He is. (1 John 3:1-2 - NKJV).

You are indeed gods, but if you don't believe me, then you will die like mere men.

Up until My time on earth, no one born of a woman was greater than John the Baptist, but the least in the kingdom is greater.

—Jesus